A Lawyer Looks at the EQUAL RIGHTS AMENDMENT

A Lawyer Looks at the EQUAL RIGHTS AMENDMENT

Rex E. Lee

Brigham Young University Press

Library of Congress Cataloging in Publication Data

Lee, Rex E   1935–
   A lawyer looks at the Equal rights amendment.

   Includes index.
   1. Sex discrimination against women–Law and
legislation–United States. 2. Women–Legal
status, laws, etc.–United States. I. Title.
KF4758.L43   342.73'0878   80-22202
ISBN 0-8425-1883-5

International Standard Book Number: 0-8425-1883-5
Brigham Young University Press, Provo, Utah 84602
© 1980 by Charles E. Jones, Trustee. All rights reserved
Printed in the United States of America
80 2.5Mp 48702

To

Janet, Diana, Wendy, Stephanie, Melissa, and Christy

Contents

Foreword

A person from Mars, come down to contemplate the development of American government from 1776 to 1980, would stand in wonder before the process we Americans use to change our written Constitution. He would marvel at a bone pile of discarded proposals, and at amendments that, by common judicial consent, have come to mean nothing. And he would shake his head at the story of our attempts to impose grand canons of equality on one another.

There is, for instance, the Fifth Amendment, part of the original Bill of Rights. At first it seemed to protect citizens from all abuses of government. But in Andrew Jackson's day the United States Supreme Court justices thought so little of the provision that they were able to hold that it protected citizens from the abuses of only the *federal* government. Later, by contrast, the justices thought so much of the Fifth Amendment that they applied most of it to local and state governments and decided that the amendment, which says nothing about equality, requires the "equal protection" of citizens. Again and again the Court amended the amendment, even though its words were never changed.

And there is the post–Civil War Fourteenth Amendment, enacted to remove what federal judges came to call "the badges of slavery." The first judges held the Fourteenth Amendment inapplicable to most of the disabilities a former slave might be expected to encounter, but later the Fourteenth Amendment came to mean that virtually the entire Bill of Rights applies against local and state governments—and even against private associations thought to exercise the powers of local and state governments. Then the "equal protection" clause of the Fourteenth Amendment was read to condemn entirely the old American system of *apartheid*–a system it had earlier been read to permit. That clause has come to abolish distinctions based on race, but at the same time to permit–and maybe even require–distinctions aimed at remedying past discrimination based on race. And, finally, it has come to mean that no level of government can, without the gravest sort of justification, distinguish between men and women. It has come to *be* an equal rights amendment.

The visitor from Mars might then drop in on political meetings devoted to discussion of the real Equal Rights Amendment, a hardy old feminist claxon that has been blaring since the 1920s. One species of discussion invokes the sorry history of the subjection of women in Anglo-American law. From this history, the visitor would learn that the time was in America—not so long ago, either—that a married woman did not in any significant sense control her own property. She could not vote, work for pay, borrow money, or practice a profession. The proposed cure—even though, given the Supreme Court's modern view of the Fourteenth Amendment, no cure is needed—is an apparently innocent, straightforward, lucid, short proposal to add an amendment to the Constitution which would forbid discrimination between the sexes. But our visitor would hear opponents of that proposal—acting from motives that are not always clear—suggest that the simple language of equality will result in a ban on rape laws and separate rest rooms for women and men, the legalization of public homosexual behavior, and the conscription of high-school girls into the infantry.

In view of such a history, and in the midst of such strident confusion, the visitor from Mars might ask, "Who can tell me, calmly, what all of this means?" And, chances are, our Republic being what it is and what it has been, someone would say, "Talk to a good lawyer." Only lawyers can be expected to understand the way Americans amend their Constitution.

Dean Rex E. Lee's book is a good lawyer's answer to the questions of a visitor from Mars. It is, of course, a brief against the Equal Rights Amendment, but there is a difference between a good lawyer's brief and a political argument. I, who have been a supporter of the amendment, and who will continue to wear my ERA bracelet, if only out of habit, am impressed and disturbed by this book. I am persuaded that supporters of the amendment should have second thoughts about their support, and that opponents of the amendment will find in it the sort of balanced, rational lawyer's assessment that their party has so often done without. But no rational reader will put it lightly aside. To his brief Dean Lee brings years of experience in the private practice of law. He brings as well the battle scars from a substantial stint as assistant attorney general of the United States, served at a time (1975-77) when the Justice Department cried out for, and occasionally got, calm, able lawyers of his integrity and rationality. He brings also the reflection of the scholar's study and of the classroom. I am grateful to him, as a colleague, for demonstrating that on some issues, and particularly the most volatile issues of public law, the country occasionally can use a few words from a law professor.

Those who have argued for the Equal Rights Amendment will learn here that the "parade of horribles" assembled against it—the consequences of the amendment for legislation on rape and rest rooms, on homosexual behavior, on conscription, and all the rest—cannot be laughed away. We *dare not* laugh at the parade and then walk away— not if we have any respect at all for history. Proponents of the ERA may have to remember, as Dean Lee has forced me to remember, that no one can predict what federal judges will do with an innocent piece of constitutional language. No sensitive person can avoid a gulp when he remembers what they *have* done with the Fifth and Fourteenth amendments and with the right-of-privacy "penumbra" they thought they found in the Bill of Rights.

Dean Lee should cause proponents to take with new seriousness this question: Is a now largely symbolic amendment to the Constitution worth the risk of providing new ammunition to judicial power, which inevitably is—because it has so often been—capricious?

Those who argue against the amendment will find this book encouraging, but they may also learn from it to lower the volume on their arguments. Proponents and opponents alike will learn the difference—a difference our legal history has honored, from Daniel Webster's generation of constitutional advocates to Rex Lee's generation—between a political argument and a good lawyer's brief.

Thomas L. Shaffer

Professor of Law, Washington and Lee University
Former Dean, Notre Dame Law School

Acknowledgments

I am grateful to my wife, Janet, and to my colleagues, Mary Anne and Steve Wood, James Backman, Reese Hansen, Lynne Wardle, and James Sabine, who read the manuscript and made valuable suggestions. Important contributions also came from my research assistants, Tom Proffitt, Ellen Dealtrey, Ken Anderson, and Dan Livingston, and from Barbara Marr, who did most of the typing.

If particular care and attention is not paid to the ladies, we are determined to foment a rebellion, and will not hold ourselves bound by any laws in which we have no voice or representation.

Abigail Adams—1776

Resolved, that woman is man's equal—was intended to be so by the Creator, and the highest good of the race demands that she should be recognized as such.

Seneca Falls Declaration of
Sentiments—1848

No State shall . . . deny to any person within its jurisdiction the equal protection of the laws.

Fourteenth Amendment—1868

Equality of rights under the law shall not be denied or abridged by the United States or by any State on account of sex.

Proposed Equal Rights
Amendment—1972

This book is about the proposed Twenty-seventh Amendment to the United States Constitution, commonly known as the Equal Rights Amendment. In a larger sense it is about women and men—women and men in the United States and the best way to achieve their interests in light of circumstances as they now exist.

The relevant circumstances today are very different from what they were in colonial/revolutionary times or at the close of the Civil War when the first constitutional guarantee of equality appeared in the Fourteenth Amendment. There is also a remarkable difference between circumstances today and in 1971, when most of the congressional hearings on the Equal Rights Amendment were held.

Colonial Period

Our early American experience was characterized by sexist attitudes, language, and discrimination.[1] The colonists arriving in Jamestown in 1607 or in Massachusetts Bay in 1628 brought with them their English legal and social traditions, including their attitude regarding the sexes. In England a woman was allowed neither to vote nor generally to serve on juries.[2] When she married, her right to own property, her right to contract, and her legal responsibility for her actions were suspended. As William Blackstone summarized the common law:

> By marriage, the husband and wife are one person in law: that is,
> the very being or legal existence of the woman is suspended
> during the marriage, or at least incorporated and consolidated into
> that of the husband.[3]

An earlier English compilation, entitled the *Lawes Resolution of Womens Rights,* explained:

> Man and wife are one person, but understand in what manner.
> When a small brooke or little river incorporateth with Rhodanus,
> Humber or the Thames, the poor rivulet looseth its name, it is
> carried and recarried with the new associate, it beareth no sway, it
> possesseth nothing during coverture. A woman as soon as she is
> married is called "covert," in Latin, "nupta," that is, "veiled," as it
> were, clouded and overshadowed, she hath lost her streame. . . . To
> a married woman, her new self is her superior, her companion, her
> master.[4]

This English common-law tradition affected the American colonial wife from the day of her marriage until the end of her life. At the moment she married, her husband gained the right to control and take the profits from her real estate; her other property became the property of her husband absolutely. The married woman could not contract, sue, or be sued; if she was harmed by another, she had to rely on her husband to sue for her. Then he, not she, became the legal owner of any awards won in the suit. If the wife committed a misdemeanor in the presence of her husband, she was relieved of criminal responsibility, which was placed on her husband. She was legally obligated to perform all domestic services such as cooking, housekeeping, bearing and rearing children, and meeting her husband's sexual demands. Her husband even had the right to discipline her. (Wife beating "with a reasonable instrument" was legal in almost every state as late as 1850).[5] In return, she was clothed, fed, and sheltered by her husband. Given today's debate over "protective legislation," it is interesting to note that Blackstone justified this discrimination against women under English common law as benign preference: "The disabilities which the wife lies under are for the most part intended for her protection and benefit: so great a favorite is the female sex of the laws of England."[6]

In the Colonials' view, the female mind was not intended for the world of ideas and strenuous mental activity. Governor John Winthrop, first governor of the Massachusetts Bay Colony, made the following entry in his journal in 1645:

> Mr. Hopkins, the governor of Hartford upon Connecticut, came to Boston, and brought his wife with him, (a godly young woman, and of special parts,) who has fallen into a sad infirmity, the loss of her understanding and reason, which had been growing upon her divers years, by occasion of her giving herself wholly to reading and writing, and had written many books. Her husband, being very loving and tender of her, was loath to grieve her; but he saw his error, when it was too late. For if she had attended her household affairs, and such things as belong to women, and not gone out of her way and calling to meddle in such things as are proper for men, whose minds are stronger, etc., she had kept her wits, and might have improved them usefully and honorably in the place God had set her.[7]

Governor Winthrop was also responsible for driving Anne Hutchinson out of the Colony for maintaining "a meeting and an assembly in your house that hath been condemned by the general assembly as a thing not tolerable nor comely in the sight of God nor fitting for your sex."[8]

A natural consequence of this attitude was that far fewer women than men received an education. In colonial New England, for example, by the time of the Revolution more than 80 percent of the men were literate, while female literacy was only 40 to 45 percent.[9] Although the Protestant doctrine that every believer should be able to read scripture dictated the early establishment of public schools in New England, they were not intended for the girls. As late as 1788, for example, the town of Northampton, Massachusetts, voted "not to be at any expense for schooling girls."[10]

Revolutionary Period

Curiously, the great liberal, egalitarian swell of the Revolution did little to change the status of women. The number of women who served as delegates to the Second Continental Congress in 1775 and the Constitutional Convention in 1787 was zero. When the great liberal Thomas Jefferson asserted in the Declaration of Independence "that all men are created equal," it was not just a slip of the revolutionary pen. For it was Jefferson who also said: "Were our state a pure democracy, there would still be excluded from our deliberations ... women, who, to prevent deprivation of morals and ambiguity of issues, should not mix promiscuously in gatherings of men."[11]

The opportunity for greater equality presented by the revolutionary circumstances did not escape the notice of at least some of the women. In 1776, while he was attending the Second Continental Congress, John Adams received this letter from his wife Abigail, just a few months before the Declaration of Independence was drafted:

> 31 March 1776: In the new code of laws which I suppose it will be necessary for you to make, I desire you would remember the ladies and be more generous and favorable to them than your ancestors. Do not put such unlimited power into the hands of the husbands. Remember, all men would be tyrants if they could. If particular care and attention is not paid to the ladies, we are determined to foment a rebellion, and will not hold ourselves bound by any laws in which we have no voice or representation.

To this, husband John replied:

> 14 April 1776: As to your extraordinary code of laws, I cannot but laugh. We have been told that our struggle has loosened the bonds of government everywhere; that children and apprentices were disobedient; that schools and colleges were grown turbulent; that Indians slighted their guardians, and Negroes grew insolent to their masters. But your letter was the first intimation that another tribe, more numerous and powerful than all the rest, were grown discontented.[12]

Presumably Adams continued to chuckle at his wife's concerns for women's rights, for neither he nor his colleagues included any mention of sex in the "new code of laws" which they later drafted and enacted. With the exception of Benjamin Franklin and Thomas Paine, whose views on the equality of women were far in advance of their time, John Adams's contemporaries generally did not believe that those "certain unalienable rights" with which all *men* are endowed by their Creator are equally bestowed upon the "other" sex.[13]

Both before and after the Revolution, the idea that women should be able to vote and hold political office was foreign to the American mind. Apparently there were no voting restrictions based on sex in the early days of the colonies, probably because no one considered that women would want to vote. Later, women were specifically excluded, starting with Virginia in 1699. After the Revolution, New Jersey, which had a constitution reading "all inhabitants," was the only state that allowed women to vote, until 1807 when it, too, excluded women from the ballot—reputedly because the legislators feared their votes.[14] In a day when suffrage was denied to a majority of the men of nearly every state, it is perhaps understandable that few protested the relegation of women to a legal status similar to that of slaves. When suffrage was broadened in later years, the privilege went first to propertyless men and then to black men, with extension to women long delayed.

Early Nineteenth Century

The turn of the century sharpened the dichotomy between the home and the economic and intellectual world outside, paralleling in the public mind the sharp contrast between the female and male natures. After his visit to the United States in 1831, Alexis de Tocqueville, in his commentaries on the young American nation, observed: "In no country has such constant care been taken as in America to trace two clearly distinct lines of action for the two sexes, and to make them keep pace one with the other, but in two pathways which are always different. American women never manage the outward concerns of the family, or conduct a business, or take a part in political life."[15]

But at the same time there was an awakening among the women of the nineteenth century. There was a rising tide of individual and organized protest against the married woman's legal subjugation to her husband, which led to the passage of the Married Women's Property Acts, beginning in Mississippi in 1839 and soon spreading to all American jurisdictions.[16] These laws generally granted married women the right to contract, to sue and be sued, to control the property they brought with them to the marriage, to be employed without their husband's permission, and to retain the earnings from their employment. Though these acts represented a great stride toward equality for married women, emancipation was hardly complete. A number of women pressed for equality in other areas.

Ironically the original inspiration for the first national women's rights convention apparently grew out of the sexist treatment of women in the antislavery movement. Lucretia Mott and Elizabeth Cady Stanton, both antislavery activists, traveled to a world antislavery convention in London in 1840. However, they were denied admission to the main hall and were relegated to a special gallery for women only. As the two returned to the United States to continue their antislavery work, their unexpected and unappreciated rebuff in London created a deep concern about the inequality betwen the sexes. In 1848 they organized the first national women's rights convention at Seneca Falls, New York, which produced the Declaration of Sentiments, a powerful statement, patterned after the Declaration of Independence, of the oppression of women. The following excerpts from this statement illustrate the intensity of feeling of the women involved and their resolve to obtain redress for years of oppression at the hands of church and state.

> We hold these truths to be self-evident: that all men and women
> are created equal; that they are endowed by their Creator with
> certain inalienable rights; that among these are life, liberty, and
> the pursuit of happiness; that to secure these rights governments
> are instituted, deriving their just powers from the consent of the

governed.... But when a long train of abuses and usurpations, pursuing invariably the same object evinces a design to reduce them under absolute despotism, it is their duty to throw off such government, and to provide new guards for their future security. Such has been the patient sufferance of the women under this government, and such is now the necessity which constrains them to demand the equal station to which they are entitled.

The history of mankind is a history of repeated injuries and usurpations on the part of man toward woman, having in direct object the establishment of an absolute tyranny over her.

... Now, in view of this entire disfranchisement of one-half the people of this country, their social and religious degradation— in view of the unjust laws above mentioned, and because women do feel themselves aggrieved, oppressed, and fraudulently deprived of their most sacred rights, we insist that they have immediate admission to all the rights and privileges which belong to them as citizens of the United States.

In entering upon the great work before us, we anticipate no small amount of misconception, misrepresentation, and ridicule; but we shall use every instrumentality within our power to effect our object.[17]

The Fourteenth Amendment

Although women activists in the early nineteenth century firmly supported the antislavery movement, when the Fourteenth Amendment was introduced in Congress in 1866, many could see that they were not to be included in the great wave of "equality." The trouble lay in the second section of the amendment, which included the word *male,* for the first time in the Constitution, in relation to the voting rights of citizens. The general guarantee of equal protection appearing in section one is not restricted to any group. But section two states that "when the right to vote ... is denied to any of the *male* inhabitants" of a state, its basis of representation in the United States Congress shall be reduced in proportion to "the number of such *male* citizens" who are denied the right to vote.[18] Ms. Stanton felt that women's suffrage would be set back a century if the amendment were adopted. Susan B. Anthony indignantly made the pledge, "I will cut off this right arm of mine before I will ever work or demand the ballot for the Negro and not the woman."[19] However, supporters of the amendment were inflamed by their thirty-five-year struggle against slavery; they were concerned with assuring the vote for the Negro, with little concern for how such a controversial measure would affect women.

In spite of the opposition of some women suffragists to section two, the Fourteenth Amendment was added to the United States Constitution in 1868. The Fourteenth Amendment is clearly the most important addition to our Constitution since the adoption of the Bill of

Rights. It is also our nation's most significant legacy from the Civil War.

The first section of the Fourteenth Amendment added three new substantive guarantees to the Constitution. They are commonly known as the *privileges and immunities* clause, the *due process* clause, and the *equal protection* clause.[20]

Prior to the enactment of the Fourteenth Amendment, neither the concept of equality, nor the words "equal" or "equality," appeared in the Constitution. The operative language of the Fourteenth Amendment guaranteeing equality is that "no State shall . . . deny to any person within its jurisdiction the equal protection of the laws." The guarantee appears to be all-inclusive, so that denials of equal protection on any basis would seem to be prohibited.

What has this constitutional guarantee of equal protection done to assure equal treatment of women?

2

The Fourteenth Amendment and Standards of Equality

Equality as a Constitutional Value

The Equal Rights Amendment would deal with equality. For three-fourths of a century the Constitution said nothing about equality. It contained neither the word nor the concept. Then in 1868 the Fourteenth Amendment became part of the Constitution, with its guarantee that "no State shall ... deny to any person ... the equal protection of the laws."

The legislative history of the Fourteenth Amendment reflects its Civil War heritage and makes it quite clear that the dominant, if not exclusive, purpose of the amendment was to assure the rights of our country's newest citizens, the newly freed slaves, members of the black race. The Thirteenth Amendment made them free, and the Fourteenth gave them other rights, including equal protection of the laws.

Nevertheless, the language of the equal protection clause does not limit its application to denials of equality on account of race. It prohibits all state-sponsored deprivations of equality, and its protections have subsequently been interpreted to apply to actions of the federal as well as state governments.[1] On its face, therefore, the Fourteenth Amendment prohibits government discrimination of all kinds, including discrimination against women.

The Fourteenth Amendment's prohibition, like that of the proposed Equal Rights Amendment, extends only to discrimination by government; it does not include discrimination by private employers, private clubs, or any other nongovernmental persons or groups. Nevertheless, there are certain categories of private conduct so identified with government that they are held to be "state action" for Fourteenth Amendment purposes.[2] Because of the similarities between the proposed Equal Rights Amendment and the equal protection clause of the Fourteenth Amendment, there is a strong likelihood that much of the state action doctrine already developed under the Fourteenth Amendment would be infused into the Equal Rights Amendment.[3]

9

The Constitution already contains, therefore, a general guarantee of equality. It prohibits governmental discrimination on all grounds, including race, sex, age, legitimacy, religion, or any other. Gender-based discriminations clearly come within its ban. Since the shelter of the equal protection clause is broad enough to cover everyone, why should any one group need its own special constitutional amendment? And if we are to carve out one group for special treatment in this respect, why should it be the members of one sex? The basic function of constitutional guarantees is to protect minority rights. One of the reasons for this protection is that by definition a minority group is one that may be unable to achieve its objectives through normal governmental processes, because it is not able to elect a majority of the lawmakers. Of the groups that have traditionally invoked the existing equal protection guarantees, all are minorities except women. Therefore, even if we were to separate one group from all of those covered by the equal protection clause, and give to that group its own individual equal protection guarantee, why should it be the only group that is not in fact a minority?

Essential to an answer to that question is an understanding of the Fourteenth Amendment's equal protection clause, particularly the standards that the courts have developed for its application in different contexts, and the history of its application—and nonapplication—to discrimination against women.

The Applicable Equal Protection Standards

The starting point for analysis of any constitutional guarantee of equality is a recognition of the reality that virtually anything government does will affect different people in different ways. Taking a literalist or absolutist view of the equal protection guarantee, consequently, would mean that most, if not all, statutes are unconstitutional.

The most important issue under the equal protection clause of the Fourteenth Amendment, the Equal Rights Amendment, or any other constitutional guarantee of equality, therefore, is the question: By what standard is the guarantee to be applied?

There are several theoretical possibilities. They can best be understood by considering them along a continuum, illustrated by Diagram A on the following page. Consider first the two extreme ends of the continuum. At one end is the absolute standard that literally any difference in treatment is a departure from the equality guaranteed by the Constitution. Discrimination is discrimination, and the Constitution prohibits all discrimination. The other absolutist view, located at the opposite end of the theoretical continuum, is that no discrimination would be unconstitutional.

No difference in treatment is unconstitutional.

Any difference in treatment is unconstitutional.

Diagram A

Neither of these standards has ever been adopted for any general category of cases under the Fourteenth Amendment. Given the broad sweep of the equal protection clause, making it applicable to all forms of discrimination, either standard would be unworkable. The absolutist position at the extreme left—that no discrimination violates—would effectively repeal any constitutional guarantee of equality. The absolutist position at the other extreme is not feasible because of the generality of the Fourteenth Amendment: since anything that government does affects some people differently than others, and since the Fourteenth Amendment prohibits all forms of discrimination, an absolutist standard at the extreme right of our hypothetical continuum would wipe out virtually all laws passed by any government.

Rational Basis. The general rule applied by the courts to Fourteenth Amendment equal protection cases is frequently referred to as the *rational basis* test. It is a test that gives significant deference to government and therefore is located toward the left side of our hypothetical continuum, as illustrated by Diagram B. The thrust of the rational basis test is that it is constitutionally permissible for government to treat people differently so long as there is some rational basis—some reason that has nothing to do with discrimination—for the difference in treatment. The practical consequence of this test is that very few governmental classification schemes subject to it will be held unconstitutional. The reason is that government usually does not enact laws solely for the purpose of discriminating against people. It follows that almost every law has some legitimate nondiscriminatory basis for the distinctions it draws, and this is all that the rational basis test requires.

No difference in treatment is unconstitutional.

Rational Basis

Any difference in treatment is unconstitutional.

Diagram B

Consider, for example, a state law requiring that all fire-department employees in the state retire at age fifty. It cannot be assumed that the sole reason for such a law is to discriminate against older people. Rather, it probably represents the lawmakers' view that older people are less able to fight fires than younger people. This legislative determination satisfies the rational basis test. The fact that some fire-fighters over fifty years of age might be more capable of fighting fires than some who are much younger is immaterial because (1) the legislature cannot be assumed to have acted from discriminatory motives in imposing the fifty-year retirement age; (2) since the legislature has to draw the line somewhere, it is entitled to draw it at any reasonable point; and (3) the fact that some individuals do not fit the general problem the legislature is attempting to solve does not affect the overall validity of the legislative solution.

The determination whether the rational basis test has been satisfied is a judicial determination, but in applying the test, courts give heavy deference to legislative judgment.[4] The net effect of applying the rational basis test, therefore, is to uphold most governmental schemes that are challenged under the equal protection clause.

Until about forty years ago, the rational basis test was the only Fourteenth Amendment equal protection standard. It is not surprising that successful equal protection challenges were extremely rare. The United States Supreme Court observed in *Buck v. Bell* that the equal protection clause is "the usual last resort of constitutional arguments."[5]

Suspect Classifications. Today there are two categories of exceptions to the rational basis standard. The first type of exception depends upon whether the individual interest affected by the discrimination is one which the Court has declared to be a "fundamental" right. The second type of exception is directly relevant to the present discussion. It is an exception that depends upon the nature of the classification.

The variety of possible bases for legislative classifications is almost limitless. Mandatory retirement laws classify on the basis of age. Highway load limit laws classify on the basis of weight. Some avocado ripeness requirement laws classify on the basis of oil content. Voter qualification laws classify on the basis of age, residence, citizenship, and sometimes literacy. Some zoning laws classify on the basis of square footage and number of occupants.

In the great majority of cases, the nature of the classification is irrelevant to the applicable constitutional standard. Rational basis, with its accompanying deference to governmental classification, is the governing rule.

However, if the legislative classification falls into any one of three classification bases that the courts have determined to be suspect classifications, then the case is taken out from under the rational basis test, and the applicable constitutional standard becomes *strict judicial scrutiny.* The phrase implies greater judicial willingness to invalidate the legislative classification, and the cases bear out this implication. The practical consequence is this: under the rational basis standard, hardly any governmental classifications that treat people differently are unconstitutional, but if the case falls under the suspect classification exception, the governmental classification will almost certainly be held unconstitutional. Thus a suspect classification shifts the constitutional standard from close to one end of the spectrum to close to the opposite end, as shown in Diagram C.

Diagram C

What, then, are these suspect classifications, whose practical effect is to transform a legislative determination from one that will probably be upheld to one that will probably be invalidated? There are three such classifications: race, national origin, and alienage. Thus, any law that treats people better or worse because of the color of their skin, or what part of the world their ancestors came from, or whether they are citizens or noncitizens,[6] is "inherently suspect" and therefore subject to strict judicial scrutiny.

In the firefighter-retirement hypothetical discussed earlier, for example, the classification basis was age: those under fifty were treated one way and those fifty and over were treated another. Since age is not one of the suspect classifications, the rational basis test applies, and the retirement scheme is constitutional. If, however, the classification basis were race, the result would certainly be different. That is, if only firefighters of a certain race were required to retire after they reached age fifty, or if the retirement program in any way treated members of one race differently from members of another, it would be unconstitutional.

What about sex as a suspect classification? Are gender-based discriminations suspect classifications, or do they come under the rational basis standard? The answer is neither. They fall somewhere in between.

3 Sex Discrimination and the Fourteenth Amendment—Privileges and Immunities and Substantive Due Process

The development of principles dealing with the constitutionality of laws treating men and women differently constitutes one of the most fascinating chapters in the history of the United States Supreme Court. Ironically it was not until 1971–103 years after equality became a recognized constitutional value, and the same year that the ultimately successful Equal Rights Amendment proposal was being debated in the Congress—that the Supreme Court for the first time in history invalidated a law on the ground that it discriminated against women.[1] Some might say that it is not ironic at all, but a matter of cause and effect that the first such decision coincided with the ERA's congressional momentum.

The Nineteenth Century Cases: Sex Discrimination and the Privileges and Immunities Clause[2]

The first cases to reach the Supreme Court involving the Fourteenth Amendment were the landmark *Slaughterhouse Cases*,[3] decided just five years after the Fourteenth Amendment became part of the Constitution. The *Slaughterhouse Cases* upheld an 1869 Louisiana law granting to the Crescent City Live-Stock Landing and Slaughter-House Company a twenty-five-year monopoly "to maintain slaughter-houses, landings for cattle and stockyards" in three parishes, including the city of New Orleans. The case did not involve sex discrimination, but its holding and rationale had a significant impact on subsequent sex discrimination cases.

The principal challenge in the *Slaughterhouse Cases* was that the statutory monopoly violated the Fourteenth Amendment's privileges and immunities clause. There was also an equal protection challenge in the *Slaughterhouse Cases*, on the obvious ground that the Crescent City Company received better treatment than the excluded slaughtering companies. The Supreme Court gave short shrift to the equal protection argument, and even more important than its holding was its rationale:

We doubt very much whether any action of a State not directed
by way of discrimination against the negroes as a class, or on
account of their race, will ever be held within the purview of this
[equal protection] provision. It is so clearly a provision for that
race and that emergency, that a strong case would be necessary for
its application to any other.[4]

The Supreme Court announced its judgment in the *Slaughterhouse
Cases* on April 14, 1873. The main significance of the judgment is the
relegation of the privileges and immunities clause to a position of rela-
tive obscurity. The Court held that "privileges or immunities of *citizens
of the United States*" are confined to those "which owe their existence to
the Federal government, its National character, its Constitution, or its
laws."[5] The pursuit of a common occupation or employment does not
qualify. This narrow definition of privileges and immunities has so se-
verely limited the application of this clause of the Fourteenth Amendment as to make it virtually impotent.[6]

Nevertheless, over the succeeding decades, litigants before the Supreme Court continued to rely on the privileges and immunities clause,
including litigants in sex discrimination cases. The day following its
Slaughterhouse decision, April 15, 1873, the Court announced its judgment in the first sex discrimination case under the Fourteenth Amendment, *Bradwell v. State.*[7] Myra Bradwell, a U.S. citizen and resident of
Illinois, had applied to the Illinois Supreme Court for a license to practice law. The Illinois Supreme Court denied her application on the
ground that an Illinois statute, as interpreted, "must operate to prevent
our admitting women to the office of attorney at law."[8]

Neither the parties nor the Court in *Bradwell* treated that case as a
sex discrimination case. Ms. Bradwell's argument that the statute was
unconstitutional did not rest on the equal protection clause nor on the
argument that she was discriminated against because she could not
practice law while men could.[9] She relied exclusively on the privileges
and immunities clause, which was the favorite of the Fourteenth
Amendment litigators during the first few decades after adoption of
that amendment. Specifically, Myra Bradwell contended that "the profession of the law, like the clerical profession and that of medicine, is
an avocation open to every citizen of the United States."[10] The excluded slaughterers in the *Slaughterhouse Cases* had contended that the
right to pursue the slaughtering business was a constitutionally protected privilege or immunity. Myra Bradwell contended the same regarding the right to practice law. In her view, her constitutional rights
had been violated not because she had been treated differently than she
would if she were a man. Rather, her position was that since she was a
citizen of the United States, she could not be foreclosed from the practice of law, which was one of the privileges or immunities of United
States citizens. The Court rejected her argument, holding that under

the *Slaughterhouse* rationale, "the right to admission to practice in the courts of the State is not one of [the privileges or immunities of citizens of the United States]."[11]

For the U.S. Supreme Court of 1873, the *Slaughterhouse Cases* presented a close question. The decision upholding the Louisiana statute was 5-4. *Bradwell,* by contrast, was not a close case for that court. The State of Illinois did not even bother to oppose Ms. Bradwell in the Supreme Court. There was only one dissent, by Chief Justice Chase, who filed no opinion.

Probably no single case has been quite as successful at incurring the wrath of women's rights advocates as *Bradwell v. State,* not only because of its holding, but even more because of the concurring opinion by Mr. Justice Bradley, in which Justices Swayne and Field joined. The opinion asserts that:

> the civil law, as well as nature herself, has always recognized a wide difference in the respective spheres and destinies of man and woman. Man is, or should be, woman's protector and defender. The natural and proper timidity and delicacy which belongs to the female sex evidently unfits it for many of the occupations of civil life. The constitution of the family organization, which is founded in the divine ordinance, as well as in the nature of things, indicates the domestic sphere as that which properly belongs to the domain and functions of womanhood. The harmony, not to say identity, of interests and views which belong, or should belong, to the family institution is repugnant to the idea of a woman adopting a distinct and independent career from that of her husband. So firmly fixed was this sentiment in the founders of the common law that it became a maxim of that system of jurisprudence that a woman had no legal existence separate from her husband, who was regarded as her head and representative in the social state; and, notwithstanding some recent modifications of this civil status, many of the special rules of law flowing from and dependent upon this cardinal principle still exist in full force in most States. One of these is, that a married woman is incapable, without her husband's consent, of making contracts which shall be binding on her or him. This very incapacity was one circumstance which the Supreme Court of Illinois deemed important in rendering a married woman incompetent fully to perform the duties and trusts that belong to the office of an attorney and counsellor.[12]

One year after *Bradwell,* the Supreme Court decided its second sex discrimination case, *Minor v. Happersett.*[13] The holding in *Minor v. Happersett,* that Missouri laws prohibiting women from voting were constitutional, affected more women, and it affected women's rights in more important ways, than the *Bradwell* decision. The Court asserted that the right to vote, even in a federal election, is not a privilege or immunity of a citizen of the United States. As in *Bradwell,* neither Virginia Minor's lawyers nor the Court dealt with the argument that her equal protection rights had been violated because Missouri permitted men, but not women, to vote.[14] The case was decided exclusively on privileges and immunities grounds.

Through the close of the nineteenth century, sex discrimination cases appear to have been argued and decided exclusively as privileges and immunities cases, and the constitutional challenges were consistently rejected. *In re Lockwood*[15] rejected the argument by Belva Lockwood, a member of the bar of the U.S. Supreme Court and several other courts, that the refusal of Virginia's Supreme Court of Appeals to admit her to practice solely because she was a woman was a denial of "a privilege or immunity belonging to her as a citizen of the United States."[16] The unanimous, brief opinion ruling against Ms. Lockwood relied on *Minor v. Happersett* and *Bradwell v. State.*

It appears that the first U.S. Supreme Court sex discrimination case in which an equal protection argument was presented to the Court was *Cronin v. Adams* in 1904.[17] The case involved a challenge by a male saloon keeper to a Denver City ordinance that prohibited women from being employed or even being present in a place where liquor was sold. The saloon keeper's lawyers relied principally on the privileges and immunities clause, though there were also some references to substantive due process and equal protection.[18] The equality-related arguments were cryptic and isolated.[19] Their principal thrust appears to be as an adjunct to the privileges and immunities argument. It was asserted, for example, that "when a Constitution guarantees to *every person* the same privileges and immunities ... it is impossible, under these constitutional limitations, to say that men may go in wine rooms, and that women may not."[20] There was one sentence, however, that contained a pure, unadulterated equal protection argument: "That no state shall pass a law which shall deny the equal protection of the laws to every citizen, applies with peculiar force to the provisions here, because, if the state can not pass such a law, a municipality can not."[21]

Whatever the thrust of Cronin's argument, it was not successful. Lawyers for the City of Denver urged that the ordinance was constitutional, and also that the male saloon keeper lacked standing to challenge it.[22] Concerning standing, counsel for the city contended: "It is a strange sort of incongruity for a saloon-keeper, who is manifestly moved by greed and cupidity, to appear in a court of conscience under the guise of defending the rights of women, when he shows that his real purpose is to do all in his power to debauch and debase her."[23]

The Supreme Court unanimously ruled that Mr. Cronin lacked standing and that, even if he had standing, "he cannot resist the ordinance."[24] Relying on its earlier holding in *Crowley v. Christensen,*[25] that "there is no inherent right in a citizen to thus sell intoxicating liquors by retail; it is not a privilege of a citizen of the State or of a citizen of the United States," the Court upheld the statute's validity.[26] The opinion contains no comment concerning the equal protection or substantive due process arguments.

Early Twentieth-Century Cases: The Due Process Clause[27]

The next significant case was *Muller v. Oregon* in 1908.[28] *Muller* is best known because it was a principal case in the leading doctrinal struggle of that era, substantive due process, and also because it was the first case in which counsel used what has come to be known as the "Brandeis brief," which goes beyond the record in the particular case and surveys general factual data relevant to the issues before the court.[29] *Muller v. Oregon* is not usually considered a sex discrimination case. It appears, however, to be the first sex discrimination case decided on a basis other than privileges and immunities. Nevertheless, it followed other traditional patterns in two respects: it was not decided under the equal protection clause, and the discrimination was held constitutional rather than unconstitutional.

Muller v. Oregon upheld the constitutionality of an Oregon statute prohibiting the employment of women "in any mechanical establishment, or factory, or laundry in this state more than ten hours during any one day."[30] All three Fourteenth Amendment guarantees—privileges and immunities, due process, and equal protection—were pressed into service in attacking the statute's constitutionality. The principal reliance, however, was on substantive due process, and on the leading substantive due process case, *Lochner v. New York,* decided in 1905.[31] *Lochner* had held that a New York law prohibiting persons from working in a bakery more than sixty hours a week or ten hours in a day deprived the parties to an employment contract of their liberty and property and was therefore unconstitutional.[32] Notwithstanding the *Lochner* precedent, the hourly limitation was upheld in *Muller* because of differences between the sexes. The Court's rationale relied upon the "potential mothers of the race" argument propounded by counsel for the state, Louis Brandeis, later a justice of the U.S. Supreme Court.

> That woman's physical structure and the performance of maternal functions place her at a disadvantage in the struggle for subsistence is obvious. This is especially true when the burdens of motherhood are upon her. Even when they are not, by abundant testimony of the medical fraternity continuance for a long time on her feet at work, repeating this from day to day, tends to injurious effects upon the body, and as healthy mothers are essential to vigorous offspring, the physical well-being of woman becomes an object of public interest and care in order to preserve the strength and vigor of the race.

Still again, history discloses the fact that woman has always been dependent upon man. He established his control at the outset by superior physical strength, and this control in various forms, with diminishing intensity, has continued to the present. As minors, though not to the same extent, she has been looked upon in the courts as needing especial care that her rights may be preserved.[33]

In *Adkins v. Children's Hospital,* decided fifteen years later in 1923, the Court reached an opposite result based on an opposite rationale.[34] *Adkins,* one of the leading cases in the now discredited line of substantive due process precedents, held unconstitutional a congressional statute that provided for the fixing of minimum wages for women and children in the District of Columbia. Applying well-known due process doctrine, the Court held that the statute was an unconstitutional infringement on property and liberty protected by the Fourteenth Amendment's guarantee against deprivations of life, liberty, or property without due process of law. The Court distinguished *Muller* mainly by rejecting its rationale that the sexes are inherently unequal:

But the ancient inequality of the sexes, otherwise than physical, as suggested in the *Muller Case* (p. 421) has continued "with diminishing intensity." In view of the great—not to say revolutionary—changes which have taken place since that utterance, in the contractual, political and civil status of women, culminating in the Nineteenth Amendment, it is not unreasonable to say that these differences have now come almost, if not quite, to the vanishing point. In this aspect of the matter, while the physical differences must be recognized in appropriate cases, and legislation fixing hours or conditions of work may properly take them into account, we cannot accept the doctrine that women of mature age, *sui juris,* require or may be subjected to restrictions upon their liberty of contract which could not lawfully be imposed in the case of men under similar circumstances.[35]

Adkins v. Children's Hospital is not usually regarded as a sex discrimination case, but in historical retrospect it is significant in this respect because it marks the first time in history that the U.S. Supreme Court invalidated a statute that treated men and women differently. (Coincidentally, the Equal Rights Amendment was first proposed to the Congress the same year as the *Adkins* decision—1923.) Arguably, it was a statute that favored women; but so-called protective legislation of the type involved in *Adkins* is frequently challenged by women's advocates, and represents the kind of legislation that would probably be unconstitutional if the Equal Rights Amendment were to become law. Indeed, in one of the two cases considered by the *Adkins* Court, the person attacking the statute was a twenty-one-year-old woman who lost her job because her employer could not afford to pay her the minimum wage.[36]

In 1937, fourteen years after *Adkins,* the Supreme Court expressly overruled it in *West Coast Hotel Co. v. Parrish.*[37] As our nation moved into the decade of the 1940s, therefore, nearly three-fourths of a century following the adoption of the Fourteenth Amendment, only once had the Supreme Court invalidated any law treating men and women differently, and that single decision had been overruled. Even more astounding is the fact that the equal protection clause not only had never been applied to a gender-based discrimination case, it had never even been considered.

4

Sex Discrimination and the Fourteenth Amendment— Equal Protection of the Laws

Drawing a Sharp Line between the Sexes

The first United States Supreme Court case to consider the constitutionality of a discrimination against women under the Fourteenth Amendment's equal protection clause was *Goesaert v. Cleary* in 1948.[1] *Goesaert* was a challenge to a Michigan statute prohibiting any woman except the wife or daughter of the male owner of a licensed liquor establishment from working as a bartender in any city having a population of over 50,000. There were two consolidated cases, brought by two groups of plaintiffs. In one case (*Goesaert*), the plaintiffs were the female owner of the bar and her daughter, both of whom worked as barmaids in the city of Dearborn. The other case (*Nadroski*) was brought by two barmaids, one of whom was also a bar owner in Detroit.[2]

The cases presented several classification bases raising possible equal protection issues. The first, and most relevant to this discussion, was the distinction between men and women: men were permitted to work as bartenders; women were not. Second, the statute distinguished between different classes of women: those who were wives or daughters of male bar owners and those who were not. This was the distinction on which the Court's brief opinion mainly concentrated. A third distinction was between barmaids and waitresses in liquor establishments, and a fourth was the classification based upon the population of the city, 50,000 or more.

For the six-man Supreme Court majority, *Goesaert* was an easy case, one that "need not detain us long."[3] Indeed, to them it was "one of those rare instances where to state the question is in effect to answer it."[4] Of the four classification bases, the only one that commanded as much as a page of discussion was the distinction between women who were and women who were not wives or daughters of male bar owners. With regard to prohibiting women from doing what men are permitted to do, the Court said:

23

Michigan could, beyond question, forbid all women from working behind a bar. This is so despite the vast changes in the social and legal position of women. The fact that women may now have achieved the virtues that men have long claimed as their prerogatives and now indulge in vices that men have long practiced, does not preclude the States from drawing a sharp line between the sexes, certainly in such matters as the regulation of the liquor traffic. See the Twenty-First Amendment and *Carter v. Virginia,* 321 U.S. 131.[5]

The dissent, authored by Justice Rutledge and joined by Justices Douglas and Murphy, concluded that the statute "arbitrarily discriminates between male and female owners of liquor establishments"[6] because while a male owner could employ his wife and daughter as barmaids, a female owner could not employ her daughter, nor could she work as a barmaid herself, even if there were a man present. The dissent did not address the broader issue, whether the statute unconstitutionally discriminated in permitting men but not women to be employed as bartenders.

The *Goesaert* case provides an excellent example of the degree of deference accorded the legislative judgment under the rational basis test. According to *Goesaert,* it was not open to an individual barmaid to prove, for example, that, in the bar where she worked, the male owner was always present and was very protective of women; whereas in the bar across the street, where the owner's daughter was employed, the owner was never present. So long as there is some reasonable basis for the legislative judgment, and so long as the legislative assumption will generally apply, the legislative classification will not be held unconstitutional. Moreover, the legislature is not required to identify the basis on which it in fact relied. Thus, Mr. Justice Frankfurter's majority opinion observes that "Michigan *evidently believes* that the oversight assured through ownership of a bar by a barmaid's husband or father minimizes hazards that may confront a barmaid without such protective oversight."[7] And the majority opinion in the three-judge district court that considered the case before it was appealed to the Supreme Court stated:

> *It is conceivable* that the Legislature was of the opinion that a grave social problem existed because of the presence of female bar tenders in places where liquor was served in the larger cities of Michigan. *It may have been* the Legislature's opinion that this problem would be mitigated . . . where there was a male licensee ultimately responsible for the condition and decorum maintained in his establishment.[8]

Women Still Regarded as Center of Home and Family Life

Hoyt v. Florida, decided in 1961, dealt with women and jury duty.[9] Florida law required that jurors be taken from "male and female" citizens having certain qualifications, but with the provision "that the name of no female person shall be taken for jury service unless said person has registered with the clerk of the circuit court her desire to be placed on the jury list."[10] In fact, only a minimal number of women registered as provided by the act, so that women rarely served as jurors in Florida. The constitutionality of the statute was attacked by a woman who had been convicted of the second-degree murder of her husband. Her husband's death occurred during an alleged altercation in which she claimed she was wounded, insulted, and humiliated to the breaking point. She seized a nearby baseball bat and ended both fight and husband, precipitating the murder prosecution. Ms. Hoyt believed that female peers on the jury would be better able to assess her plea of temporary insanity. Her constitutional claim was that her trial before an all-male jury, under an overall scheme whose practical effect was to exclude women from jury service, violated her Fourteenth Amendment rights. It was not really an equal protection question, but rather one of procedural due process. The Court concluded that there had been no purposeful discriminatory exclusions from jury service and affirmed her conviction. In justifying Florida's jury-selection scheme, the Court returned to a familiar theme: "Despite the enlightened emancipation of women from the restrictions and protections of bygone years, and their entry into many parts of community life formerly considered to be reserved to men, woman is still regarded as the center of home and family life."[11]

Hoyt v. Florida was explicitly overruled in 1975 by *Taylor v. Louisiana*:[12] "If it was ever the case that women . . . were so situated that none of them should be required to perform jury service, that time has long since passed."[13]

A Perceptible Change

The pivotal case in the history of the U.S. Supreme Court sex discrimination precedents is *Reed v. Reed,* decided in 1971.[14] It was the first Supreme Court decision to hold that a classification based on sex violates the Fourteenth Amendment's equal protection clause. *Reed v. Reed* also figured prominently in the Equal Rights Amendment hearings, which were held after the Supreme Court had agreed to take the case but before the opinion was handed down.[15] ERA proponents asserted, as one of their principal arguments, that the amendment was needed because the Supreme Court had never held the equal protection clause applicable to sex discrimination cases and was not likely to do so.[16] The decision in *Reed v. Reed* necessarily modified that assertion.

Reed v. Reed involved a dispute between the separated adoptive parents of Richard Lynn Reed, a minor who had died in 1967 without leaving a will. Both parents sought appointment to administer the son's estate. The Idaho court appointed the father, apparently on the sole basis of an Idaho statute providing that, "of several persons claiming and equally entitled to administer, males must be preferred to females."[17] The Supreme Court's opinion holding the statute unconstitutional was short and unanimous. The governing judicial standard appears to have been the traditional one, rational basis. Thus the Court noted:

> The question presented by this case, then, is whether a difference
> in the sex of competing applicants for letters of administration
> bears a rational relationship to a state objective.[18]

The opinion also contained, however, at least a suggestion that a different test might apply; the Court observed that the Idaho statute, by providing for different treatment on the basis of sex "establishes a classification *subject to scrutiny* under the Equal Protection Clause."[19]

Neither the words *suspect classification* nor *strict judicial scrutiny* were employed by the opinion. And the Court's statement of the question clearly imported a rational basis approach. But the other words, *subject to scrutiny,* are not rational basis words, and at least opened the door to the possibility of greater scrutiny for classifications based on sex than the simple inquiry of whether or not they are reasonable. As important as it was, therefore, *Reed v. Reed* left uncertain the issue of the governing standard. Was it to be rational basis, or strict judicial scrutiny?

The answer proved to be neither.

Almost a Suspect Classification

The high-water mark for suspect classification/strict judicial scrutiny advocates came a year after *Reed* in *Frontiero v. Richardson.*[20] Sharron Frontiero, a lieutenant in the U.S. Air Force, was married to a full-time college student, Joseph Frontiero. Lieutenant Frontiero claimed her spouse as a dependent in order to obtain the increased quarters allowance and other housing and medical benefits allowed to dependents of members of the uniformed services. Under the governing federal statutes, a serviceman was entitled to claim his wife as a dependent without having to prove that she in fact depended upon him for support. In contrast, a servicewoman was not entitled to claim her husband as a dependent unless she proved that in fact she provided more than one-half of his support. Lieutenant Frontiero therefore claimed that, since the burden of proof was placed upon female but not male members of the uniformed services, the statute clearly created a distinction based on sex.

By a vote of eight to one the U.S. Supreme Court held the statute unconstitutional under the Fifth Amendment.[21] The real significance of *Frontiero v. Richardson,* however, is that the Court was just one vote shy of the majority (five of the nine) necessary to declare that sex is a suspect classification. *Frontiero* has been misunderstood by some people in this respect. There was no "opinion of the Court" in *Frontiero.* That means that, while eight members of the Court agreed that Sharron Frontiero was entitled to win her case, five members could not agree on the governing reason. The principal opinion in the case (sometimes called the plurality opinion), authored by Mr. Justice Brennan and joined by Justices Douglas, White, and Marshall, adopts the suspect classification test: "At the outset, appellants contend that classifications based upon sex, like classifications based upon race, alienage, and national origin, are inherently suspect and must therefore be subject to close judicial scrutiny. We agree."[22] Relying on the "subject to scrutiny" language of *Reed v. Reed,* the plurality opinion asserted: "We . . . find at least implicit support for [the strict judicial scrutiny] approach in our unanimous decision only last Term in *Reed v. Reed.*"[23] This opinion was not elevated to the level of a principle of constitutional law, however, because it failed to command the needed five-vote majority.

Mr. Justice Powell wrote a concurring opinion, joined by Chief Justice Burger and Justice Blackmun, arguing that it was unnecessary to reach the suspect classification issue, because Lieutenant Frontiero was entitled to win in any event on the authority of *Reed v. Reed.* Justice Powell's opinion further adds:

> There is another, and I find compelling, reason for deferring a general categorizing of sex classifications as invoking the strictest test of judicial scrutiny. The Equal Rights Amendment, which if adopted will resolve the substance of this precise question, has been approved by the Congress and submitted for ratification by the States.[24]

The Current Standard

So what is the current test? It is not rational basis. But neither is it strict judicial scrutiny. It lies somewhere between the two, requiring more judicial scrutiny than rational basis but more deference to governmental classification than strict judicial scrutiny. The case that established the current test was *Craig v. Boren.*[25] Both the facts of that case and the language of the opinion demonstrate that the prevailing test lies somewhere between rational basis and strict judicial scrutiny.

Craig v. Boren was an equal protection challenge brought by a male, contending that an Oklahoma statutory scheme prohibiting the sale of "nonintoxicating" 3.2 percent beer to males under twenty-one and to females under eighteen violated his equal protection rights. The Supreme Court held that the Oklahoma distinction worked as an unconstitutional denial of equal protection to men between the ages of eighteen and twenty. This time there was an opinion of the Court (five justices concurring), written by the author of the *Frontiero* plurality opinion, Mr. Justice Brennan. Once again, the majority relied on the "subject to scrutiny" language of *Reed v. Reed*—not strict judicial scrutiny but simply *judicial scrutiny.*

Another phrase that implies about the same standard as strict judicial scrutiny is *compelling state interest.* Compelling state interest, like strict judicial scrutiny, almost invariably results in unconstitutionality. A phrase used by the majority in *Craig v. Boren* is similar, but again implies a somewhat less demanding standard: "To withstand constitutional challenge previous cases establish that classifications by gender must serve *important governmental objectives* and must be *substantially related* to the achievement of those objectives."[26]

Thus, to survive a rational basis test, a statutory classification must merely be *rationally* related to the achievement of a *legitimate* governmental objective. To withstand strict judicial scrutiny, a classification must be *necessary* to the accomplishment of a *compelling state interest.* To withstand judicial scrutiny since *Craig v. Boren,* a gender-based classification must be *substantially* related to the achievement of an *important* governmental objective.

The facts in *Craig v. Boren* demonstrate as distinctly as the language of the opinion that the Court's test is something beyond rational basis. The 1973 arrest statistics for persons in the eighteen- to twenty-year-old age group in Oklahoma showed that the number of alcohol-related offenses was substantially higher for males than females. For driving under the influence of alcohol, the number was 427 males compared with 24 females, and for drunkenness, 966 males and 102 females.[27] The Court's opinion points out that the difference in male and female arrests also exists at older ages.[28] This aspect of the opinion serves to underline the significant differences between the *Craig v. Boren* test and rational basis. Under the rational basis test, the fact that there was also a disparity between male and female alcohol-related offenses in age groupings other than eighteen to twenty-one amounts only to an underinclusiveness argument: that the legislature has not attempted to solve all of the problems at once. Under the rational basis test, it is not a sufficient equal protection argument that the statute is under-inclusive.[29] Rational basis permits government to carve out any portion of the problems that it perceives and deal with them one at a time. If rational basis had been the test, therefore, the State of Oklahoma could have treated men and women in the eighteen to twenty-one age range differently, on a showing that alcohol-related problems in that age range were greater for males than females. The fact that they were also greater for males than females in some other age range where the state did not differentiate would have been immaterial.

Other cases subsequent to *Craig v. Boren* have reaffirmed the location of the constitutional standard for sex discrimination somewhere between rational basis and strict judicial scrutiny. It is probably closer to strict judicial scrutiny, as shown on Diagram D, but there is little question that it falls short of being a full-fledged suspect classification. For example, while it is extraordinarily rare that the courts will ever uphold any legislative classification based on race, the Supreme Court in sex classification cases has ruled for government in a substantial number of cases.[30] (See Appendix A for an annotated list of cases in each category.)

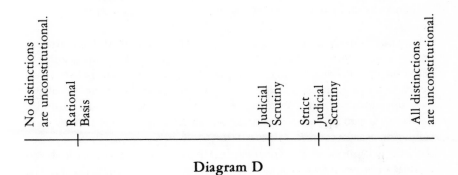

Diagram D

Under any constitutional test, one of the issues concerns the closeness of the fit between what the legislature is attempting to achieve and the means that it has selected to achieve it. In other words, how likely is it that what the legislature did will in fact solve the problem? Will the means achieve the end? The prevailing approach in equal protection cases governed by rational basis is to give the legislature every benefit of the doubt. Recall, for example, the District Court's standard in *Goesaert,* that "it is conceivable."[31] Though the difference is not subject to accurate measurement, it is clear to me that the Court's intermediate level of scrutiny for sex discrimination cases—requiring a "substantial relationship" between the governmental objective and the statute drafted to achieve it—demands a closer fit between means and end than under the rational basis test. Cases supporting this conclusion are: *Califano v. Westcott,*[32] *Caban v. Mohammed,*[33] *Orr v. Orr,*[34] and *Weinberger v. Wiesenfeld.*[35]

What about "reverse" or "benign" discrimination, statutes favoring women? The broader issue of reverse discrimination, as it applies not only to gender classifications but also to others, particularly those involving race, is discussed in Chapter 14 of Rex E. Lee, *With Liberty for All: A Study of the United States Constitution* (Provo, Utah: Brigham Young University Press, forthcoming). It is noteworthy that although the most famous reverse discrimination cases have involved race, the principles of constitutional law have been better developed in the sex discrimination area.[36] The Court has not yet attempted any definitive statement, but I believe it can be fairly concluded from the Court's opinions that:

1. If the favoritism toward women in fact represents a benign discrimination, that is, a legislative attempt to compensate for past discriminatory acts against women, then the classification will be upheld.[37]

2. If, on the other hand, the favoritism toward women is based on what the Court has termed archaic notions concerning women's place in society, and what is and is not acceptable for women to do, then the scheme is likely to be invalidated.[38]

The Fourteenth Amendment had been part of our Constitution for 36 years before anything resembling an equal protection argument was even made before the U.S. Supreme Court, 40 years before a sex discrimination case was decided on any ground other than privileges and immunities, and 55 years before any Supreme Court case invalidated a gender-based classification on any grounds (and this invalidation was overruled 15 years later). It was not until 1948, 80 years after the adoption of the Fourteenth Amendment, that a gender-based classification was attacked in the Supreme Court principally on the ground that it violated the Fourteenth Amendment's equal protection clause, and that argument was summarily dismissed. Not until 1971, 103 years after the general guarantee against governmental deprivations of equality was written into the Constitution, did the Supreme Court apply that guarantee to invalidate a state scheme that treated men and women differently.

Appendix A contains a summary of the facts and holdings of most U.S. Supreme Court cases dealing with sex discrimination. A review of those cases is instructive for several reasons. First, the body of law is rather well developed and sophisticated. A nonissue for over a century, Fourteenth Amendment sex discrimination cases over the last nine years have been one of the hot spots of constitutional adjudication.

Second, unlike the standards on either side of it, the test governing gender-based discrimination has no strong predisposition either favoring or disfavoring government. Rational basis implies that so long as there is some reason for the discrimination, it will be upheld. And that is the way the standard has been applied. Strict judicial scrutiny, by contrast, imports an intensity of review that few schemes can survive. Judicial scrutiny is different. The words suggest no tilt in either direction, and this neutrality has been reflected in the results. Judicial scrutiny is a tool that not only permits but also requires courts to give careful consideration to each instance in which government treats women and men differently.

The third observation is necessarily subjective, but I believe it is substantially accurate. Taking the decisions in their entirety, I believe they represent what the majority of American citizens would consider about the right result. Clearly, some people will agree and some will disagree with individual decisions. Some will feel that as a whole the cases have gone too far, and others that they have not gone far enough. But most, I suspect, would conclude that the center of gravity is about where it ought to be. Several American experiences of recent years—most notably the exclusion of women from draft registration in 1980—suggest that the national mood does not favor radical changes in limiting government's flexibility to treat women and men differently.

Probably the most remarkable fact about the body of constitutional law dealing with sex discrimination is that all the development has occurred within less than a decade. It is little wonder that in the early 1970s, when the Congress of the United States began to hold the hearings that ultimately resulted in congressional passage of the Equal Rights Amendment, the proponents of equal rights for women had despaired of any constitutional help ever coming from the Fourteenth Amendment.

History of the
Equal Rights Amendment

The United States Constitution presently contains one amendment dealing with women's rights. Adopted in 1920, the Nineteenth Amendment provides that "the right of citizens of the United States to vote shall not be denied or abridged by the United States or any State on account of sex." The amendment is one of the three that reversed specific decisions of the United States Supreme Court. The decision reversed by the nineteenth was *Minor v. Happersett*.[1] If the equal protection clause of the Fourteenth Amendment had been applied before 1920 the same way it is today, the Nineteenth Amendment clearly would have been unnecessary.

The Early Experience

During the struggle to obtain the vote, women from all political persuasions unified their efforts to secure ratification of the Nineteenth Amendment. The focal point of that unity was the struggle for suffrage, but once the vote was obtained, the common ground—and with it feminist unity—ceased to exist.[2] The traditionally more conservative National American Women's Suffrage Association, which subsequently became the League of Women Voters, considered the Nineteenth Amendment as substantially establishing equality for women. The more radical National Women's Party[3] viewed suffrage for women as only the first step of a long journey[4] and believed that a constitutional amendment was the only reasonable way to shorten that journey. Thus, spearheaded by Alice Paul, the National Women's Party sought adoption of the Equal Rights Amendment as a corollary to the Nineteenth Amendment. In 1923, three years after the Nineteenth Amendment became part of the Constitution, the Equal Rights Amendment was first introduced in Congress. Identical resolutions were introduced in the United States Senate and House by Senator Charles Curtis and Representative Daniel Anthony (a nephew of Susan B. Anthony), both of Kansas.[5]

The language of the 1923 version was different from that which successfully emerged from Congress a half-century later, though both were short and full of ambiguity. The 1923 version provided:

> Men and women shall have equal rights throughout the
> United States and every place subject to its jurisdiction.
> Congress shall have power to enforce this article by
> appropriate legislation.[6]

After its initial introduction, resolutions proposing an Equal Rights Amendment were introduced in every succeeding Congress, including the Ninety-second Congress in 1971.[7] Additionally, twelve congressional hearings on the amendment were held between 1924 and 1971.[8] However, it was not taken seriously until after the Second World War, during which women were called upon to do much of what had formerly been considered men's work.[9]

In 1943 the Senate Judiciary Committee first reported favorably on the ERA resolution.[10] That Committee's favorable report continued in every Congress from the Seventy-eighth (1943) through the Eighty-eighth (1964).[11] In 1946 the language of the proposed amendment was changed to read:

> Equality of rights under the law shall not be denied or
> abridged by the United States or by any State on account of sex.
> Congress and the several States shall have power, within their
> respective jurisdictions, to enforce this article by appropriate
> legislation.[12]

In 1950 the Senate approved the Equal Rights Amendment resolution by a vote of 63 to 19[13] and approved it again in 1953 by a vote of 73 to 11.[14] However, both times the amendment passed the Senate only after being amended by the following language proposed by Senator Hayden: "The provisions of this article shall not be construed to impair any rights, benefits, or exemptions conferred by law upon persons of the female sex."[15] In the view of the ERA proponents, this "Hayden rider" effectively nullified the proposed amendment.[16] The purpose of the amendment was to eliminate distinctions between men and women, and the Hayden rider perpetuated the open-ended possibility that judges could draw such distinctions.

In 1963 the ERA was dealt another blow. On October 11, the President's Commission on the Status of Women, established by President Kennedy in 1961, issued its final report, which stated in part:

> Since the Commission is convinced that the U.S.
> Constitution now embodies equality of rights for men and
> women, we concluded that a constitutional amendment need not
> now be sought in order to establish this principle. But judicial
> clarification is imperative, in order that remaining ambiguities

with respect to the constitutional protection of women's rights be
eliminated.

Early and definitive court pronouncement, particularly by the
U.S. Supreme Court, is urgently needed with regard to the validity
under the 5th and 14th amendments of laws and official practices
discriminating against women, to the end that the principle of
equality become firmly established in constitutional doctrine.[17]

By 1970, however, because hopes were running out that the Fifth
and Fourteenth amendments would be applied as suggested,[18] efforts to
obtain a separate constitutional amendment were vigorously renewed.[19]

Congressional Consideration and Approval

Resolutions calling for an Equal Rights Amendment were introduced in the Ninety-first Congress by Representative Martha Griffiths and Senator Eugene J. McCarthy.[20] This time the proponents were
determined that there would be no equivalent of the Hayden rider.[21]

Hearings were held by the Senate Judiciary Committee's Subcommittee on Constitutional Amendments on May 5, 6, and 7, 1970[22]
and by the full judiciary committee on September 9, 10, 11, and 15,
1970.[23] Prior to completion of the Senate hearings, on August 10, 1970
the House approved the amendment by a vote of 352 to 15.[24] The Senate, after extended debate, added what they called "perfecting amendments" exempting draft laws, imposing a seven-year time limit on ratification, and changing the effective date from one year after ratification
to two.[25] They also attached a rider dealing with prayers in public
buildings.[26]

The proposal was then laid aside and it appeared it would be defeated by lack of action. In what the *New York Times* described as an
"effort to revive the nearly dead Equal Rights Amendment,"[27] Senator
Birch Bayh offered a revised version whose crucial language keyed the
amendment to "equal protection"—the more familiar phrase found in
the Fourteenth Amendment—rather than "equal rights."[28] The most ac-
tive opposition to the Bayh Amendment came from ERA proponents,
who protested that it would permit legislatures and courts to find compelling reasons for certain classifications, and this result was unaccept-
able.[29] In spite of Senator Bayh's efforts, the Ninety-first Senate took no
further action on the equal rights measure, simply allowing it to die
quietly. This marked the third time that the Equal Rights Amendment
had passed one house of Congress only to die in the other.[30]

The successful congressional effort was initiated in 1971 with the
introduction of resolutions calling for an Equal Rights Amendment by
Representative Martha Griffiths and Senator Marlow Cook.[31] There was
one substantive change to the proposed amendment, whose language
had remained essentially the same from 1946 to 1970.[32] That change

granted to Congress exclusive jurisdiction to enforce the proposed amendment.[33] Previous proposals had split the enforcement jurisdiction between the federal government and several states.[34]

Additional hearings were held on March 24, 25, and 31, and April 1, 2, and 5, 1971, before Subcommittee 4 of the House Judiciary Committee.[35]

In the Ninety-second Congress, as in the Ninety-first, a major strategic issue involved amendments—amendments ERA proponents were determined to avoid. The prevailing view among congressional proponents was that "to be at all effective a constitutional amendment must be in the form ... originally introduced."[36] Following the conclusion of the hearings, the House Judiciary Subcommittee, as in the case of the Senate hearing the year before, reported the measure to their full judiciary committee. In a close nineteen-to-sixteen vote, the judiciary committee added a section proposed by Congressman Wiggins providing that the amendment would "not impair the validity of any law of the United States which exempts a person from compulsory military service or any other law of the United States or any State which reasonably promotes the health and safety of the people."[37]

On October 12, 1971 the House of Representatives rejected the Wiggins amendment by a vote of 265 to 87[38] and then approved the Equal Rights Amendment in its original form by the overwhelming margin of 354 to 24.[39] The battle thereupon shifted back to the Senate.

Six weeks after House approval, on November 22, 1971, the Senate Subcommittee on Constitutional Amendments adopted by a vote of six to four the following substitute language for the entire amendment.

> Section 1. Neither the United States nor any State shall make any legal distinction between the rights and responsibilities of male and female persons unless such distinction is based on physiological or functional differences between them.
> Section 2. The Congress shall have the power to enforce the provisions of this article by appropriate legislation.[40]

Three months later, on February 29, 1972, the matter came before the full Senate Judiciary Committee, which rejected the subcommittee's substitute by roll-call vote of fifteen to one.[41] The Senate report explained that the judiciary committee agreed with Professor Thomas Emerson of the Yale Law School that "the Ervin Amendment [the one adopted by the Senate Subcommittee] would nullify the whole purpose of the Equal Rights Amendment. More than that it would put women in a worse position than they are now."[42] The Senate Judiciary Committee also rejected five other amendments proposed by Senator Ervin.[43] Then, on March 14, 1972, the judiciary committee reported the original resolution favorably,[44] and eight days later the Equal Rights Amendment passed the Senate by a vote of eighty-four to eight. The amendment now having passed both houses of Congress, it was sent to the states for ratification.[45]

Ratification, Rescission, and Extension

Literally within hours of the final Senate vote, Hawaii became the first state to ratify. Twenty-one additional states ratified during 1972: Alaska, California, Colorado, Delaware, Idaho, Iowa, Kansas, Kentucky, Maryland, Massachusetts, Michigan, Nebraska, New Hampshire, New Jersey, New York, Pennsylvania, Rhode Island, Tennessee, Texas, West Virginia, and Wisconsin. Eight more states joined the ranks in 1973: Connecticut, Minnesota, New Mexico, Oregon, South Dakota, Vermont, Washington, and Wyoming. Three more followed in 1974: Maine, Montana, and Ohio. North Dakota ratified in 1975. There were no ratifications in 1976, and the final state to ratify, the thirty-fifth, was Indiana in January 1977.[46]

During the hearings before the House subcommittee, proponents had expressed confidence in quick ratification among the states,[47] and the first year's experience seemed to bear out that optimism. Indiana's ratification in 1977, the thirty-fifth ratifying state, left the ERA only three states short of the necessary two-thirds majority. However, for each of the three years following 1972 the number of ratifying states was about a third of what it had been during the preceding year: 22, 8, 3, 1. And failure of quick ratification was accompanied by a further, damaging, complication. Five legislatures voted to rescind their previous ratifications. Nebraska rescinded first, on March 15, 1973.[48] Tennessee followed in 1974,[49] Idaho in 1977,[50] Kentucky in 1978,[51] and South Dakota in 1979.[52]

Article V of the United States Constitution provides for amendments. The process is a difficult one, requiring concurrence by two-thirds of the members of both houses of Congress and ratification by the legislatures of three-fourths (currently thirty-eight) of the states.[53] What is the present status of the Equal Rights Amendment? Do the five rescinding states count or not?[54] The Supreme Court has held that a state legislature which has initially rejected a proposed constitutional amendment may later approve it,[55] but it has never definitively ruled on the converse—whether a state may change its view from yes to no before the constitutionally required consensus of three-fourths of the state legislatures has been reached.

How long do the proponents of a constitutional amendment have to obtain the required three-fourths approval by the states? In *Dillon v. Gloss,* the Supreme Court ruled: "Of the power of Congress, keeping within reasonable limits, to fix a definite period for the ratification we entertain no doubt."[56] Beginning with the Eighteenth Amendment, adopted in 1919, that is exactly what Congress has done with each proposed constitutional amendment—prescribe the period within which it must be ratified. With the Eighteenth, Twentieth, Twenty-first, and Twenty-second amendments, Congress made the seven-year limitation a part of the constitutional amendment itself.[57] Beginning with the Twenty-third, however, in order to avoid unduly lengthening the Constitution, the time limitations became part of the preambles to the amendments.[58] This same pattern was followed with respect to the Equal Rights Amendment.[59]

The specified seven-year period for the ERA expired on March 22, 1979. As of that date, only thirty-five states had ratified, including the rescinding states, which at that time included only four. However, on October 6, 1978 Congress took an unprecedented step: it extended the time for ratification. On that date the Senate voted (60 to 36) to extend the seven-year time limitation by three years, thereby concurring in the House's previous decision (233 to 189) of August 15, 1978.[60] In neither the House nor the Senate did the extension vote command a two-thirds majority. The Equal Rights Amendment's new lease on life runs to June 30, 1982.

The legality of extension, like rescission, has never been passed upon by the U.S. Supreme Court. Both issues are now pending in a suit filed in the United States District Court for the District of Idaho.[61]

6

What Would the ERA Do?
The Uncertainty of the Standard

Few issues in this generation have produced as much emotion as the Equal Rights Amendment. Unfortunately, the debate has been responsible for more heat than light. Many of the proponents have asserted that this is a simple amendment, that it does nothing more than guarantee that government must treat women fairly and give them the same rights as men. Who could possibly oppose fair and equal treatment for women?

The opponents, by contrast, assert that the ERA will result in a "parade of horribles," including everything from legalized rape and prostitution to sexually integrated public restrooms to single men and women sleeping together in state college dormitories.

Who is right? Equally important, because the predictions of both sides are so far apart, and because the ERA has been such a divisive issue, why can not someone definitively clarify what its results will be?

There is a single answer to both of these questions. It is impossible for anyone to predict with confidence what the ERA really means—either during the present period before ratification or, if ratified, for decades thereafter. If adopted, the Equal Rights Amendment will be one of those constitutional provisions that is cast in such broad terms that the only way its meaning can be ascertained is by adjudication. Some constitutional amendments are fairly precise, so that there is comparatively little need, or opportunity, for judicial interpretation. Examples are the Seventeenth (direct election of senators), the Twenty-second (limiting the office of president to two terms), and the Twenty-sixth (eighteen-year-old vote). The language of others (the Fourteenth is a classic example) is so broad that the interpretation process extends literally over centuries and in fact never ends. The language breadth of the Equal Rights Amendment fits it in this latter category, the same category as the Fourteenth. Its meaning, therefore, will be determined over a period of many decades as actual lawsuits—cases and controversies involving application of the Twenty-seventh Amendment—work their way up through the courts. It is the courts, as they decide those cases, that will shape the meaning of the amendment, pouring specific content into it on a case-by-case basis.[1]

Therefore, whether there will be a parade of horribles, and if so, how horrible the parade will be, are questions that no one can answer now. Even more important, both sides in the debate are missing the real point: since there is a possibility that some of the disadvantages feared by its opponents could become a reality, do the advantages of the amendment outweigh the risks? What is needed is a cost/benefit analysis—a comparison of how much we gain and how much we give up. On the gain side, the question is: What would the ERA yield in terms of needed equality for women that is not already afforded by existing law, or that could not be achieved without a constitutional amendment? On the cost side: What is the likelihood that some or all of the consequences predicted by the opponents will become a reality, and if they do, how detrimental would these consequences be?

The opening question in the analysis of either costs or benefits is: How high is the constitutional hurdle that governmental distinctions between men and women would have to clear under the Equal Rights Amendment?

Recall the continuum of possible standards for constitutional guarantees of equality (Diagram D, Chapter 4, page 29). At this time (1980), under the Fourteenth Amendment's equal protection clause the applicable standard for sex discrimination is judicial scrutiny. Both the language of that test and the way in which the courts have applied it indicate that it is something less than the strict judicial scrutiny applicable to suspect classifications.

What standard would govern legislative distinctions between men and women under the Equal Rights Amendment? We will consider four possibilities: (1) that the standard would remain exactly where it is under the Fourteenth Amendment; (2) that sex, like race, would become a suspect classification, subject to strict judicial scrutiny; (3) that the standard would be absolute, permitting no governmental distinctions of any kind between men and women; and (4) that the standard would be absolute, but subject to certain qualifications.

These four possibilities are not listed in the order of intensity of their judicial scrutiny. Listing them in that order would reverse numbers 3 and 4 because the absolute standard with no exceptions would result in the greatest judicial invalidation of legislative decisions. This is shown by Diagram E. Discussion and analysis are aided, however, by considering the absolute standard before the absolute standard with qualifications. The four standards are therefore examined in the order listed, rather than in the order of degree of change they would bring to existing law.

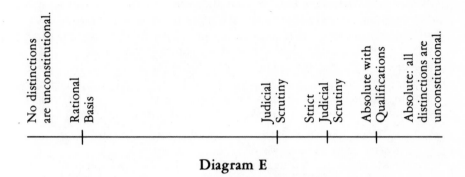

No distinctions are unconstitutional.

Rational Basis

Judicial Scrutiny

Strict Judicial Scrutiny

Absolute with Qualifications

Absolute: all distinctions are unconstitutional.

Diagram E

No Change From Existing Law: Judicial Scrutiny

The likelihood that the Equal Rights Amendment would make no difference in the existing standard for sex discrimination is slight. There is a general principle governing the interpretation of constitutional provisions, and of laws in general, that the addition of a new provision to an existing body of law will be interpreted in such a way that it adds something to what is already there.[2] Otherwise, why the additional provision? It seems a fair assumption that this principle would be applied to the ERA. It is a virtual certainty, therefore, that the wattage on the constitutional searchlight will be turned up from judicial scrutiny. The real question is, how high?

Suspect Classification Subject to Strict Judicial Scrutiny

This one is a possibility. It finds some support in the history of congressional consideration of the proposed amendment[3] and in one opinion of three United States Supreme Court justices.

Many of the proponents—probably a majority—who testified at the congressional hearings did not focus on what kind of standard would apply if the amendment were adopted. At the time of the hearings, no Supreme Court case had ever held any governmental discrimination based on sex unconstitutional,[4] and the principal thrust of the testimony at the hearings was that the constitutional guarantee of equality should be extended to women.[5] The language used by many of the proponents, however, seems most consistent with the view that sex classifications would be treated the same as race classifications.[6] The fair inference to be drawn is that the speakers assumed that the standard of judicial review would be the same as for racial classifications: strict judicial scrutiny.

In 1973 at least three members of the U.S. Supreme Court believed that passage of the Equal Rights Amendment would move sex discrimination cases into the suspect classification category. The case was *Frontiero v. Richardson.*[7] The issue in that case, it will be recalled, was whether strict judicial scrutiny should apply to sex discrimination cases. Four justices answered that question in the affirmative. However, three other justices, although they agreed that Frontiero should win her case, disagreed as to the reason. The concurring opinion written by Justice Powell, joined by Chief Justice Burger and Justice Blackmun, gives the following as one of the reasons for *not* making sex a suspect classification under the Fourteenth Amendment's equal protection clause:

> There is another, and I find compelling, reason for deferring a general categorizing of sex classifications as invoking the strictest test of judicial scrutiny. The Equal Rights Amendment, which if adopted *will resolve the substance of this precise question,* has been approved by the Congress and submitted for ratification by the States. . . . It seems to me that this reaching out to pre-empt by judicial action a major political decision which is currently in process of resolution does not reflect appropriate respect for duly prescribed legislative processes.[8]

"This precise question" which, in Justice Powell's view, the ERA would resolve, is whether the "strictest test of judicial scrutiny" should be applied.

The issue of the applicable ERA standard would ultimately be decided by the Supreme Court. Accordingly, any expressions on this issue by members of that Court are entitled to significant weight. However, the concurring opinion in *Frontiero* was joined by less than a majority, and there is reasonable doubt whether any of the three concurring justices would still be on the Court when and if the issue of the governing ERA standard is presented.[9] Some limited support for a strict judicial scrutiny standard might also be found in the interpretation placed on the Texas Equal Rights Amendment by that state's Court of Civil Appeals.[10]

An Absolute Standard: No Constitutionally Permissible Governmental Distinctions between Men and Women

This is the standard at the extreme right of the hypothetical continuum. It would permit no governmental distinctions between men and women—none whatever.

The stereotypical view of men and women held by some people is that men have one set of physical, intellectual, and emotional equipment that fits them for certain kinds of activities, and that women are physically weaker, more timid, more emotional, more tender, and more in need of protection from the brutal realities of life. (Recall Justice

Bradley's opinion in *Bradwell.*)[11] The advocates of an absolutist (or qualified absolutist) approach to the Equal Rights Amendment consider the persistence of this stereotype as the root cause of discrimination against women. If women are to achieve their rightful place, they believe the stereotype must be rooted out. Women must be seen not as members of a stereotypical group, but as individuals, some married, some single, some short, some tall, some tender and emotional, some stoic. They consider the only adequate vehicle for such a task to be a constitutional amendment. Moreover, the destruction of the stereotype must be complete. There can be no exceptions, because past experience has shown that exceptions open the door for the return of the stereotype.

Of all the standards, the absolute approach would be the easiest to understand and to apply. The reason is simply that no governmental distinctions between men and women would be permitted. The changes that it would require would be enormous. This is the standard that would make the parade of horribles an unquestionable reality.

The support for an absolutist position comes from two principal sources: the language of the amendment and congressional rejection of qualifying amendments offered by Senator Ervin and Congressman Wiggins.

The Language of the Amendment. On its face the Equal Rights Amendment permits no exceptions or qualifications and leaves no room for flexibility, no matter how compelling the circumstances. Section 1 states, "Equality of rights under the law shall not be denied or abridged by the United States or by any State on account of sex." The language is not even limited to distinctions between men and women. One of the amendments proposed by Congressman Wiggins and rejected by the House would have eliminated this ambiguity.[12]

Ironically, one argument against applying the amendment exactly as it reads is provided by the equal protection clause of the Fourteenth Amendment. If that guarantee were applied as it reads, all legislation drawing any distinction of any kind would be unconstitutional, and that would mean almost all laws would be unconstitutional.

The Ervin and Wiggins Amendments. By a nineteen-to-sixteen vote the House Judiciary Committee adopted two amendments proposed by Congressman Wiggins to House Joint Resolution 208,[13] which had introduced the ERA in the House. The first of these amendments added the words "of any person" in the first section, so that section read, "Equality of rights of any person under the law shall not be denied or abridged by the United States or by any State on account of sex." The purpose of this amendment was to eliminate any doubt that the ERA applied only to human beings. The second amendment added a new section:

This article shall not impair the validity of any law of the United States which exempts a person from compulsory military service or any other law of the United States or of any State which reasonably promotes the health and safety of the people.[14]

The nineteen-member majority felt the amendment was necessary because of the confusion emanating from "the fact there [was] widespread disagreement among the proponents of the original text of House Joint Resolution 208 concerning its legal effects."[15] While some proponents argued that the original language would permit reasonable classifications, "other proponents argue strenuously that the use of the word 'equality' in the original text is intended to assure that men and women are given 'identical' legal treatment."[16] The reason that the majority members favored the second Wiggins amendment was that they believed it would establish strict judicial scrutiny as the governing standard. Without the amendment, they feared that the absolute language of House Joint Resolution 208 would be interpreted as it read.[17] Thus, the second of the Wiggins qualifying amendments was needed to prevent possible unwanted interpretations:

> The rigidity of interpretation advocated by many of the proponents of the original text of House Joint Resolution 208 could produce a number of very undesirable results. For example, not only would women, including mothers, be subject to the draft but the military would be compelled to place them in combat units alongside of men. The same rigid interpretation could also require that work protective laws reasonably designed to protect the health and safety of women be invalidated; it could prohibit governmental financial assistance to such beneficial activities as summer camp programs in which boys are treated differently than girls; in some cases it could relieve the fathers of the primary responsibility for the support of even infant children, as well as the support of the mothers of such children and cast doubt on the validity of the millions of support decrees presently in existence. These are only a few examples of the undesirable effects that could be produced by the enactment of the original text of House Joint Resolution 208.[18]

The minority members of the House Judiciary Committee opposed the Wiggins amendments, principally because they opposed any amendments. They took the position of the qualified absolutists. They agreed with Professor Emerson that "the original text [of the ERA] is based on the fundamental proposition that sex should not be a factor in determining the legal rights of women or of men."[19] The Wiggins amendment, they said, "does violence to the concept of equality itself."[20]

The full House rejected the Wiggins amendments, 265 to 87.[21]

Senator Ervin of North Carolina proposed several amendments to the ERA before the Senate Judiciary Committee and its Subcommittee on Constitutional Amendments. All were eventually defeated by the judiciary committee. Those amendments dealt with such matters as exempting women from the draft, exempting women from military combat, extending protections to wives, mothers, or widows (presumably in matters such as property tax exemptions, child support, alimony, and the like), securing rights of privacy "to men or women, or boys or girls" and making "punishable as crimes rape, seduction, or other sexual offences."[22]

Senator Ervin tried several approaches. Before the Senate subcommittee he proposed an exemption for distinctions "based on physiological or functional differences between [male and female persons]."[23] The full Senate Judiciary Committee rejected the subcommittee's adoption of this amendment, on the ground that it would "nullify the whole purpose of the Equal Rights Amendment."[24] Senator Ervin then proposed to the full committee one amendment listing rather specifically a number of distinctions to which the Equal Rights Amendment would not apply. The language of that amendment was:

> The provisions of this article shall not impair the validity, however, of any laws of the United States or any State which exempt women from compulsory military service, or from service in combat units of the Armed Forces; or extend protections or exemptions to wives, mothers, or widows; or impose upon fathers responsibility for the support of children; or secure privacy to men or women, or boys or girls; or make punishable as crimes rape, seduction, or other sexual offenses.[25]

When the judiciary committee rejected this amendment, Senator Ervin offered four more, each of which had a narrower scope, and each of which was also rejected. Those amendments were:

> Nothing contained in this article shall be construed to deprive the United States and the several States of the legislative power to extend to female persons any right or protection sanctioned by the fifth or fourteenth articles of amendment.

> This article shall not impair the validity of any law of the United States which exempts women from compulsory military service or service in combat units of the Armed Forces.

> This article shall not impair the validity of any law of the United States which exempts women from compulsory military service.

> No federal law shall prohibit an institution of higher education from enrolling only male or female students or students of both sexes. If any such institution of higher education enrolls both male and female students, such institution shall not be allowed to accept only a certain percentage of individuals of either sex.[26]

The strongest case for the significance of the proposal and rejection of these amendments can be simply stated: If those who voted for the Equal Rights Amendment did not intend it to repeal rape laws or require that women be sent into combat, then why did they reject amendments stating that, in those and other instances, the broad language of the amendment does not mean what it says?

There are other possible explanations for rejection of the Wiggins and Ervin amendments. First, the proponents brought their measure to Congress in the early 1970s with the conviction that the earlier "Hayden riders" attached to the Senate-passed versions of 1950 and 1953 had effectively nullified their constitutional amendment. They were determined that this would not happen again. There was, simply, a categorical resistance to language changes of any kind.[27] Second, while the broader Ervin amendment based on "physiological and functional differences" was characterized as effectively nullifying the ERA, there is language in the legislative history describing the more specific amendments as "unnecessary" because, "as previously explained, the Equal Rights Amendment will not require that fathers be relieved of their responsibilities for support of children ... nor will it interfere with the constitutional right to privacy ... nor will it invalidate State laws punishing rape or other sexual crimes based on unique physical characteristics of one sex."[28]

How persuasive is this explanation that the rejected clarifying amendments were unnecessary? The explanation has some persuasive force but is far from conclusive. Statements made by individual members of Congress or even committee reports are far less indicative of the true legislative intent of a constitutional amendment than of a statute. A constitutional amendment is a product of fifty-one different legislatures, of which Congress is only one. The majority members of the Senate Judiciary Committee who authored Senate Report Number 92-689 may have felt that the unqualified language of the Equal Rights Amendment was really subject to qualifications. But there is no indication that every member of the House and Senate who voted for it shared those same views. There is even less assurance that legislators in Nebraska, Delaware, Oregon, or any other ratifying state read that language the same way. Under those circumstances, the fact that Congress rejected the proposed amendments retains considerable persuasive force.

Senator Ervin warned of the possibility of an absolutist interpretation and supported his view with the opinions of two of this country's foremost scholars, Professors Paul Freund and Philip Kurland. The views of these two scholars are contained in responses to questions by Senator Ervin and published in the Senate report:

> Senator Ervin. And if the House-passed equal rights
> amendment were ratified by the states, thus made a part of the

Constitution, it is susceptible of interpretation that would require the courts to strike down all legal distinctions made between men and women, no matter how reasonable and necessary those might be?

Mr. Freund. That is my understanding of what the language as well as the purpose of the sponsors is today.[29]

Professor Kurland. I would think that the amendment as it is now simply provides that classification by sex by any governmental action is invalid.

Senator Ervin. In other words, your interpretation of the amendment as presently phrased is that it would be probably interpreted to eliminate sex as a basis for classification in legislation?

Professor Kurland. If I were charged with the interpretation of the language, that would be the conclusion that I would reach.

Senator Ervin. If that interpretation would be correct, the law which exists in North Carolina and virtually every other state of the Union which requires separate restrooms for boys and girls in public schools would be nullified, would it not?

Professor Kurland. That is right, unless the separate but equal doctrine is revived.[30]

Other scholars, most notably Professor Thomas Emerson (see discussion in following section), disagree with the general view that the ERA absolutely would forbid all gender-based discrimination and specifically that it would ban separate public restrooms. These matters will be discussed in greater detail in Chapters 7 through 10.

Probably the most persuasive arguments against the likelihood of an absolutist standard are, first, that none of those who testified in favor of the ERA before the Congress advocated such a standard; and second, that only a small minority of today's population, including judges, would really favor the extreme consequences of such a standard.

Absolute Standard with Qualifications

An absolute standard subject to qualifications finds support in the legislative history and in state court decisions interpreting state constitutional provisions following the same model as the proposed federal ERA.

Legislative History. The strongest support in the legislative history for this standard is contained in testimony by Professor Thomas Emerson of the Yale Law School.[31] Professor Emerson also gives the clearest statement of the rationale for an absolutist position. It is a rationale apparently shared by many ERA proponents.

In essence, the rationale is that the only way to achieve true equality for men and women is to make no exceptions. Permitting government to treat men and women differently, whether under the rubric of rational basis, or compelling state interests, or strict judicial scrutiny, or anything else, simply will not work. History has proven that it will not work. Even laws that purportedly favor women end up being used as tools to discriminate against them. The only way to assure equality, therefore, is to do it completely. Professor Emerson observed that "the failure of [ERA] proponents ... to formulate a clear theory of the amendment and its application has confused consideration of the issues and left us without a satisfactory legislative history."[32]

The governing premise, in Professor Emerson's view, should be:

> Sex should not be a factor in determining the legal rights of women, or of men. The existence of a characteristic found more often in one sex than the other does not justify legal treatment of all members of that sex different from all members of the other sex. The same is true of the functions performed by individuals. The circumstance that in our present society members of one sex are more likely to be found in a particular type of activity than members of the other sex does not authorize the Government to fix legal rights or obligations on the basis of membership in one sex. The law may operate by grouping individuals in terms of existing characteristics or functions, but not through a vast overclassification by sex.
>
> The main reason underlying this basic concept derives from both theoretical and practical considerations. The equal rights amendment embodies a moral value judgment that a legal right or obligation should not depend upon sex but upon other factors—factors which are common to both sexes. This judgment is rooted in the basic concern of society with the individual, and with the right of each individual to develop his own potentiality.[33]

Applying this basic theory, Professor Emerson's standard is:

> From this analysis it follows that *the constitutional mandate should be absolute.* The issue under the Equal Rights Amendment cannot be benefit or detriment, reasonable or unreasonable classification, strict scrutiny, compelling reasons, or the demands of administrative expediency. *Equality of rights simply means that sex is not a factor.*[34]

In Professor Emerson's judgment, "no exceptions are necessary or desirable."[35] However, he advocates two "qualifications."[36]

The first qualification is that "the equal rights amendment does not preclude legislation, or other official action, which relates to a physical characteristic unique to one sex." Emerson makes it rather clear that this qualification has a very short reach. By his own characterization, "instances of laws directly concerned with physical differences found only in one sex are relatively rare."[37] The clearest examples include laws relating to wet nurses and regulating the donation of sperm.[38] There are also some other examples, however, that in his view come within this first qualification:

> Instances of laws directly concerned with physical differences found only in one sex are relatively rare. Yet they include many of the examples cited by opponents of the equal rights amendment as demonstrating the nonviability of that proposal. Thus not only would laws concerning wet nurses and sperm donors be permissible but so would laws establishing medical leave for child bearing, though medical leave for child rearing would have to apply to both sexes. Laws punishing forcible rape, which relate to a unique physical characteristic of man, would remain in effect. So would paternity legislation. Laws dealing with homosexual relations would likewise be unaffected, for such laws also deal with physical characteristics pertaining only to one sex.[39]

The second qualification was described as follows:

> A second qualification of the central principle of the equal rights amendment flows from the constitutional right of privacy, established by the Supreme Court in *Griswold v. Connecticut,* 381 U.S. 479 (1965). Thus the right of privacy would justify police practices by which a search of a woman could be performed only by another woman and search of a man by another man. Similarly the right of privacy would permit, perhaps require, the separation of the sexes in public restrooms, segregation by sex in sleeping quarters of prisons or similar public institutions, and a certain segregation of living conditions in the Armed Forces. It is impossible to spell out in advance the precise boundaries that the courts will eventually fix in accommodating the equal rights amendment and the right of privacy. In general it can be said, however, that the privacy concept is applicable primarily in situations which involve disrobing, sleeping, or performing personal bodily functions in the presence of the other sex. The great concern over these matters expressed by opponents of the equal rights amendment seems not only to have been magnified beyond all proportion but to have failed to take into account the impact of the young, but fully recognized, constitutional right of privacy.[40]

What is the difference between "exceptions," which Emerson contends the amendment will not permit, and the two "qualifications" which he contends are applicable? His testimony before Congress and the Yale Law Journal article he co-authored lead to the conclusion that exceptions would be genuine departures from the general principle of absolute equality that Emerson believes constitutes the indispensable foundation stone of the Equal Rights Amendment. The two qualifications, by contrast, theoretically do not involve departures from this principle. The first, physical characteristics unique to one sex, is simply a recognition that the guarantee of absolute equality between men and women has no applicability to laws that are keyed to characteristics unique to men or to women. Sperm donor laws can apply only to men, and wet nurse laws and laws allowing medical leave for child bearing can apply only to women. Restricting those kinds of laws to one sex does not really discriminate at all, and the first qualification leaves intact the purity of the general principle that the Equal Rights Amendment is absolute in its ban on sex distinctions.

Analysis of the second qualification is more sophisticated. So is the task of preventing the qualification from shading over into exceptions. According to the argument, the Equal Rights Amendment, as part of the Constitution, must be integrated with other constitutional principles. Among these is the right of privacy, declared by the Supreme Court in *Griswold v. Connecticut* and other cases.[41] With the side-by-side existence of two constitutional principles—the absolute ban on any distinctions between men and women contained in the Equal Rights Amendment, and the right of privacy declared by the Supreme Court—the two must be accommodated when they come into conflict. In Professor Emerson's view, therefore, nonapplicability of the Equal Rights Amendment to matters of individual privacy does not involve exceptions to the ERA's absolute prohibitions; it is simply a matter of accommodating different constitutional guarantees.

The problems caused by the attempt to apply these two qualifications to some of the contexts to which Professor Emerson contends they apply will be discussed in Chapter 8.

The views of Professor Emerson concerning the interpretation of the Equal Rights Amendment are entitled to greater weight than would normally be accorded a law professor. The same views that he advanced in the congressional hearings were developed in greater detail in a Yale Law Journal article which he co-authored.[42] Senator Ervin quoted Senator Bayh, a leading ERA proponent, as having described that article as a "masterly piece of scholarship," and Congresswoman Griffiths, the amendment's principal sponsor in the House of Representatives, as having characterized it as one that will "help you understand the purposes and effects of the ERA."[43] Since Senator Bayh and Congresswoman Griffiths are both leading proponents of the ERA, their favorable characterization of the article—particularly the congresswoman's statement that it is one that will "help you understand the purposes and effects of the ERA"—makes more persuasive Professor Emerson's views concerning its meaning. Fourteen members of the House Judiciary Committee, all proponents, stated that the ERA's "basic premise ... is ... as stated by Professor Thomas Emerson that sex should not be a factor in determining the legal rights of women or men."[44]

The Yale Law Journal article was probably the single most frequently cited document appearing in the congressional legislative history.[45] At least five state supreme courts have cited it as the primary support for their standard of judicial review.[46] The article also contains the most carefully developed statement of rationale supporting a national Equal Rights Amendment, and a qualified absolutist interpretation of that amendment if adopted. It is cited frequently throughout the remainder of this book and for convenience is referred to as the "Yale Law Journal article."

State Court Interpretations of State Equal Rights Amendments. To date, sixteen states have included provisions in their constitutions providing some measure of equality based on sex.[47] Nine of these states have adopted provisions essentially the same as the proposed Twenty-seventh Amendment to the United States Constitution.[48] Several others have used equal protection language.[49] In at least five states (Maryland, Pennsylvania, Washington, Colorado, and Hawaii), state courts have used absolutist language in deciding cases under their constitutional provisions, all of which are similar to the national ERA. In some of those cases the courts have used absolutist language without qualification.[50] In the really hard cases, however, involving rape,[51] homosexual marriages,[52] and topless bathing suits,[53] the courts have relied on the unique physical characteristics qualification in holding the statute to be constitutional.[54]

Probably the three leading state Supreme Court cases are *Rand v. Rand*,[55] *Henderson v. Henderson*,[56] and *Darrin v. Gould*.[57] In *Rand,* the Maryland Supreme Court established the standard of judicial review for that state's Equal Rights Amendment as follows:

> The words of the E.R.A. are clear and unambiguous; they say
> without equivocation that "Equality of rights under the law shall
> not be abridged or denied because of sex." This language
> mandating equality of rights can only mean that sex is not a
> factor.[58]

The Maryland Court of Special Appeals in *Coleman v. Maryland*[59] has interpreted the *Rand* test as requiring that under the Maryland Equal Rights Amendment all distinctions based on sex "are now absolutely forbidden."[60]

The Pennsylvania Supreme Court in *Henderson v. Henderson* stated:

> The thrust of the ERA is to insure equality of rights under the
> law and to *eliminate sex as a basis for that distinction.* The *sex* of the
> citizens of this Commonwealth *is no longer a permissible factor* in
> the determination of their legal rights and legal responsibilities.
> The law will not impose different benefits or different burdens
> upon the members of a society based on the fact that they may be
> a man or a woman.[61]

Darrin v. Gould held that refusal by a school district to permit two sisters to play on the high school football team violated Washington's Equal Rights Amendment. Among the facts reviewed by the Washington Supreme Court's opinion were: "Carol and Dolores Darrin were students at the Wishkah Valley High School in Grays Harbor County, Washington, during the fall of 1973. Carol was then a junior, 16 years of age, 5'6" tall, weighing about 170 lbs. Dolores was then a freshman, 14 years of age, 5'9" tall, weighing about 212 lbs. They wished to play contact football. The high school had no girls' football team."[62]

The high school coach was willing, indeed apparently anxious, to use the girls. The only reason he did not do so was that regulations of the Washington Interscholastic Activities Association prohibited girls from participating in interscholastic contact football on boys' football teams. The Washington Supreme Court observed that the governing test under the Equal Rights Amendment went beyond either rational basis or strict scrutiny. The Court also cited with approval the statement by the Yale Law Journal: "The guarantee of Equal Rights for women may not be qualified in the manner that [suspect classification] or [fundamental interest] doctrines allow."[63]

At least one lower Washington court has read *Darrin v. Gould* to mean that "the [ERA] provision is an *absolute prohibition* against discrimination based on sex."[64] A concurring opinion in *Darrin v. Gould* stated:

> With some qualms I concur in the result reached by the majority. I do so, however, exclusively upon the basis that the result is dictated by the broad and mandatory language of [the Washington ERA]. Whether the people enacting the ERA fully contemplated and appreciated the result reached, coupled with its prospective variations may be questionable. Nevertheless, in sweeping language they embedded the principle of the ERA in our constitution, and it is beyond the authority of this court to modify the people's will. So be it.[65]

From this review of the supporting arguments for four alternative judicial standards under the Equal Rights Amendment, the only clear conclusion is no conclusion. It is impossible for any fair-minded person to state with confidence that any of these four standards will emerge victorious. The first alternative—no change at all—is highly unlikely, and the governing standard will probably be located somewhere along the continuum to the right of its present location. How far to the right? That is a matter that, under our constitutional system, adoption of the Equal Rights Amendment would necessarily place in the hands of the courts. It is a question that the courts may not answer for decades. It is even possible that the question would be answered by future

Supreme Court justices not yet in law school, perhaps not yet born, when the great national debate over the ERA was raging.

It is against the background of undeniable uncertainty concerning its governing standard that the probable impact of the Equal Rights Amendment in different substantive areas must be assessed.

7   The Equal Rights Amendment, the Draft, and Combat

There is little doubt that if the Equal Rights Amendment becomes law, men and women will be equally subject to compulsory military service whenever compulsory military service is in effect. I know of no disagreement with this proposition expressed by any person who testified at the congressional hearings, or by any responsible commentator. Whether mothers with small children must also be drafted and whether women must serve in combat units on the same basis as men are less clear.

Women and the Draft

The issue is not whether Congress is to have the power to draft women. Congress has that power under existing law. Rather, the issue is whether Congress *must* draft women in the event that it drafts men. Under the ERA the answer to that question is unmistakably yes.

As stated by the Senate report:

> It seems likely that the ERA will require Congress to treat men and women equally with respect to the draft. This means that, if there is a draft at all, both men and women who meet the physical and other requirements, and who are not exempt or deferred by law, will be subject to conscription.[1]

At a convention in March 1971 the Intercollegiate Association of Women Students (IAWS) adopted a resolution expressing the view that "the major issue concerning the equal rights amendment is the question of women's involvement with the draft."[2] This statement by IAWS also reflects another frequently expressed view, which almost welcomes extension of the draft to women. One reason is its possible assistance in eradicating stereotypical notions about women and what they can do. The IAWS resolution states, for example, "Resolved that given whatever selective service prevails, IAWS supports the involvement of women equally with men in the responsibilities, requirements, and rights inherent in that system."[3] Virginia R. Allan, former chairman of the President's Task Force on Women's Rights and Responsibilities, stated, "I cannot put words in their mouths but, from the interpretation I received from listening to them, these young women are willing to do anything the young men are willing to do."[4] Similarly, Jean Faust, former president of the New York chapter and member of the National Board of the National Organization for Women (NOW), testified:

> There is an understanding among people that women are not to
> serve their country, that women are to serve individuals—that is,
> husbands and families, and I deeply regret that exclusion of
> women from the greater society—where it is not considered proper
> that women serve their country.[5]

Some of the proponents see the effect of the draft on the stereotype as more than symbolic. Many people share the view that those who are susceptible to military service take citizenship obligations more seriously and have a greater stake in matters of politics and government. This is reminiscent of President Eisenhower's non sequitur of a quarter century ago supporting the eighteen-year-old vote: "If they're old enough to fight, they're old enough to vote." A more sophisticated but related idea was stated by Norman Dorsen, president of the American Civil Liberties Union, at the congressional hearings:

> On a deeper level, when women are excluded from the
> draft—the most serious and onerous duty of citizenship—their
> status is generally reduced. The social stereotype is that women
> should be less concerned with the affairs of the world than men.
> Our political choices and our political debate often reflect a belief
> that men who have fought for their country have a special
> qualification or right to wield political power and make political
> decisions. Women are in no position to meet this qualification.[6]

In a similar vein, the Yale Law Journal article states: "Having served or being liable to serve also tends to make an individual sensitive to and concerned about the country's foreign policy."[7]

Drafting Mothers of Small Children

What about drafting mothers with small children? The answer to this question is not as clear. Under a qualified absolute standard, no preference could be given mothers because such a preference would not come within either the unique physical characteristics qualification nor the privacy qualification. During the congressional hearings, the following exchange occurred between Congressman Wiggins and Mr. Dorsen:

> Mr. Wiggins. Would it be appropriate to not draft women
> with small children and, at the same time, draft men with small
> children?
> Professor Dorsen: I don't think so.[8]

The Yale Law Journal article agrees and suggests several alternatives for deferment in the case of small children, including, "Whichever parent was called first might be eligible for service; the remaining parent, male or female, would be deferred."[9]

The Senate majority report takes the position that mothers with children would not be subject to the draft.[10] In assessing the comparative weights of a Senate majority report on the one hand, and on the other the testimony of one witness at a hearing and a law review article, the former would normally be more persuasive. It may not be in this instance. The Senate majority report has a conciliatory tone; its apparent purpose was to persuade reluctant colleagues that Senator Ervin's strident dissent was overstated. Moreover, if the qualified absolutists are correct,[11] then many of the statements contained in the Senate majority report are simply inconsistent with the underlying theory of the Equal Rights Amendment.

Women in Combat

What about combat? Would the ERA compel military leaders to use women in combat, or would it leave the option to use them or not? Here the answers are less clear. Many ERA proponents who testified during the congressional hearings either avoided the issue or handled it as delicately and ambiguously as possible. The Senate majority report, for example, stated: "Once in the service, women, like men, would be assigned to various duties by their commanders, depending on their qualifications and the service's needs."[12] The report also stated: "In Israel, women are required to serve in the Defense Forces just as men. They are not, however, assigned to combat posts."[13] This statement concerning the Israeli experience is contradicted by some of the testimony at the hearings.[14]

The Nixon administration was also evasive of the combat issue. William H. Rehnquist, then an assistant attorney general and now a Supreme Court justice, appeared before the House subcommittee representing the Nixon administration. He declined to give definitive answers to some questions but later responded in writing, at the request of Chairman Edwards, congressman of California and one of the principal proponents. With respect to the military, Mr. Rehnquist—as other witnesses before and after him—skirted the hardest question: whether the military would be required to use women in combat. He phrased the issue in terms of whether women must be *permitted* to volunteer:

> The question here is whether Congress would be required either
> to draft both men and women or to draft no one. A closely
> related question is whether Congress must permit women to
> volunteer on an equal basis for all sorts of military service,
> including combat duty. We believe that the likely result of

passage of the equal rights amendment is to require both of these results.[15]

Virginia Allan, former chairman of the President's Task Force on Women's Rights and Responsibilities, pointed out that in the past, nurses had been involved in combat duty.[16] Several witnesses noted that there might be instances in which women were not suited for combat,[17] without really coming to grips with the ultimate issue whether, aside from individual differences, the amendment would require that men and women, as groups, be treated equally with respect to combat duty.

Another theme of some of the witnesses was that women were capable of handling combat and would be better at it than many people would think.[18] Although he did not personally favor women in combat, Professor Dorsen observed: "There are some people who would say I am wrong and that women should go into combat in the United States as they did in the underground in France, as they do in the Israeli army, and as they do in the Vietnamese army."[19]

The absolutists were not ambiguous on this issue. The purity of their position is not only consistent with, but is required by, the basic theory that in their view undergirds the entire amendment. The Yale Law Journal article states: "Women will serve in all kinds of [military] units, and they will be eligible for combat duty."[20] With respect to women's abilities and women as combat troops, and the possible brutalizing effect of combat on them, the article states:

> Women in other countries, including Israel and North Vietnam, have served effectively in their armed forces. There is no reason to assume that in a dangerous situation women will not be as serious and well disciplined as men.
> Finally, as to the concern over women engaging in the actual process of killing, no one would suggest that combat service is pleasant or that the women who serve can avoid the possibility of physical harm and assault. But it is important to remember that all combat is dangerous, degrading and dehumanizing. That is true for all participants. As between brutalizing our young men and brutalizing our young women there is little to choose.[21]

In the event women are susceptible to combat duty, there are other problems that are largely nonquantifiable. First is the problem of additional facilities for women. Former Assistant Secretary of Defense Don R. Brazier said, when the ERA was being debated in Congress:

> Until a definitive plan is developed indicating where and under what circumstances women would serve in isolated areas, with com-batant forces, aboard ships, etc., it is not possible to make a definitive estimate of costs. If extensive additional facilities or modifications to current facilities were required, the costs could be considerable.[22]

Second, even if segregation of living quarters and facilities is allowed under the amendment, during combat duty in the field there are often virtually no facilities at all, and privacy for both sexes might be impossible to provide.

Third is the problem of "nonmilitary attachments." For example, the military is reluctant to assign brothers to the same combat units because there are strong nonmilitary attachments involved that can interfere with the performance of military duty in combat. Similarly, men and women have the tendency to form strong nonmilitary attachments that in combat might cause concern.

Women's leaders have long considered the military one of the great bastions of discriminatory attitudes and practice. The military has always imposed rather rigid quotas on the numbers of women who are permitted to serve in certain positions in the military. Additionally, the laws of many states give hiring and other preferences to veterans, and this has had the necessary effect of incorporating into state law the consequences of military discrimination.[23]

Although important steps have been taken in recent years to upgrade the status of women in the military—such as increased occupational-specialty opportunities for women, promotion of women to general and flag rank, and the opening of the service academies to woman officer aspirants—there is still need for greater equality.

The authors of the Yale Law Journal article expressed the view that the Equal Rights Amendment "will require a radical restructuring of the military's view of women, which until now has been a narrow and stereotypical one."[24] For this reason, those authors applaud the fact that:

> The Equal Rights Amendment will have a substantial and pervasive impact upon military practices and institutions. As now formulated, the Amendment permits no exceptions for the military. Neither the right to privacy nor any unique physical characteristic justifies different treatment of the sexes with the respect to voluntary or involuntary service, and pregnancy justifies only slightly different conditions of service for women.[25]

With respect to the three issues treated in this chapter, there is little doubt that the Equal Rights Amendment would subject women to the draft.[26] Few issues concerning the amendment are as clear. Conscription of mothers with small children and service in combat are less clear. They fall into the same area as do most Equal Rights Amendment issues: it is impossible to give a confident conclusion before passage of the amendment and judicial interpretation.

Sex Offenses, Public Sleeping, and Homosexual Conduct

Mandatory repeal of all rape laws. Men and women sleeping in the same rooms in prisons, state college dormitories, and military barracks. Mandatory repeal of all laws prohibiting homosexual conduct, including homosexual marriages. These possibilities march in the front rank of the parade of horribles. They also share another common characteristic: advocates of the absolute standard—subject to the qualifications of unique physical characteristics and right to privacy[1]—have identified each of the possibilities as fitting within one or the other of the qualifications. In other words, it is their position that, under their view of the Equal Rights Amendment, laws in all three of the possibilities would survive. Is this position correct?

Once again, no one can answer that question with certainty. In my opinion, the answer turns on the governing constitutional standard. If it is strict judicial scrutiny, I would agree with the proponents that passage of the ERA will probably not require invalidation of laws prohibiting forcible rape, homosexual relations (including marriage), and cohabitation by unmarried persons of publicly owned sleeping facilities. If absolutism is the test, all three kinds of laws will be unconstitutional. If the test is qualified absolutism tempered by the two qualifications of unique physical characteristics and right to privacy, then forcible rape laws have a chance for survival, but laws in the other two possibilities are squarely inconsistent with the qualified absolutist theory. If laws in those categories survive such a standard, it will be only because practical considerations outweigh underlying doctrine.

The arguments in support of the different possible standards have already been discussed. This chapter is devoted to a discussion of why laws dealing with consensual sex offenses (including homosexual conduct) and with coeducational public sleeping facilities are incompatible with the absolutist standard, why they are not saved by either of the qualifications, and why forcible rape laws raise serious questions under the qualified absolutist test.

The qualified absolutists, led by Professor Emerson, attempt to save rape and homosexual laws under the aegis of the first qual-

61

ification—unique physical characteristics—and laws requiring segregated public sleeping facilities under the second—right to privacy.

Laws Prohibiting Rape

The legislative history contains a number of assurances that the Equal Rights Amendment, if passed, would not invalidate laws prohibiting forcible rape.[2] None of the proponents of the amendment want it to nullify forcible rape laws. How, then, can it be seriously suggested that the amendment might have this effect? The answer is that if the qualified absolutist position becomes the law, then there is a strong argument that rape laws cannot withstand the theoretical demands of that standard, the proponents' preferences notwithstanding. (Such an argument could be made by a person convicted under a law prohibiting rape.)

Forcible rape is defined by the Model Penal Code,[3] and by the laws of some states, as sexual intercourse by a man with a female not his wife, without her consent.[4] Thus, the rape laws of these states apply only to men. This could be cured by broadening the laws to prohibit, as many states have done,[5] any unwanted forcible sexual activity. The issue, however, is the constitutionality of rape laws as they presently exist.

In support of their position that rape comes within the first qualification, unique physical characteristics, the Yale Law Journal article argues:

> All or nearly all women's genitals differ from all or nearly all
> men's genitals in that they can be penetrated in an act of sexual
> assault against the victim's will. Rape laws could thus be sustained
> as a legislative choice to give one part of the body (unique to
> women) special protection from physical attack.[6]

This argument links present rape laws aimed only at men with the "unique physical characteristics" qualification. It is clear that the identification of physical penetration as the harm that rape laws seek to eradicate is the reason for its suggested inclusion within the first qualification. The Yale Law Journal article further states:

> By contrast, the statutes which include penetration "per anum and
> per os" in the definition of rape, could not justifiably be limited
> to female victims because no physical characteristic unique to
> women is being protected by these laws. A court could choose
> between invalidating these broader rape laws or else limiting them
> to penetration of a woman's genitals.[7]

The vulnerability of this argument is the narrowness of the assumption that rape laws are aimed at physical invasions of one part of the human body, unique to women, by another part of the human body, unique to men. The more realistic assumption is that the purpose of rape laws is not just to prevent unwanted physical penetration, but the unwanted total impact on the human psyche. The emotional damage is much more severe than the physical. Indeed, there was testimony to this effect during the congressional hearings. When asked if child molesting by a male should be taken any more seriously than child molesting by a female because of the possibility of pregnancy, one witness answered: "I see no difference. The horror of the crime is to me, if I were to weight it one way or the other, I would be more horrified, I think, that a mother would molest a child, given her relationship with the child as we envision it should be, than with the father."[8]

Forcible rape laws are similar. For some in our society, preservation of premarital virginity and avoidance of extramarital sex relations are moral values of the highest order. Violation of those values, which are just as important to men as to women, can result in severe emotional impact whose magnitude knows no gender-based distinctions. Some may say that, like the stereotype of women, such values are based on outmoded notions. But that misses the point. Outmoded or not, they are important values to the people who hold them. The inability of state legislatures to use their best judgment in protecting against intrusion on such values would diminish individual dignity and liberty. There are other people for whom, though they do not consider extramarital sex a moral issue, sexual assault inflicts enduring emotional damage wholly aside from whether there is physical penetration and wholly aside from whether the victim is a man or woman. Fitting forcible rape laws which follow the Model Penal Code prototype within the unique physical characteristics exception is based on the proposition that the purpose of those laws is to prevent a physical intrusion of which only men are capable. This is a narrow, unrealistic view of rape laws and of the objectives of the legislatures that enacted them. For this reason, the attempt to save them under the qualified absolutist standard is subject to serious question.

I recognize that, notwithstanding the theoretical inconsistencies, a court that wanted to uphold forcible rape laws under the qualified absolutist standard could do so by seizing upon the unique physical characteristics qualification. Indeed, there would be strong practical reasons to do so, though the practical considerations might not be adequate to overcome the doctrinal inconsistencies.

Whether or not existing rape laws were held unconstitutional, it is unlikely that rape would go unpunished. Even if the legislatures did not act quickly to enact new rape laws, the offense could be punished as an assault under the laws of most states, though the punishments might not be as severe as under the rape laws.

What of sexual offenses other than forcible rape? The qualified absolutists make no claim that laws dealing more harshly with men than with women with respect to such matters as statutory rape[9] or incest[10] would survive under their test. They are sex discriminatory and fall within neither qualification. Many prostitution laws providing punishment for female prostitutes but providing no punishment for male prostitutes or for men who purchase the services of female prostitutes have already been amended to make them sex neutral; ERA would almost certainly invalidate those that remain.[11]

Homosexual Conduct, Including Homosexual Marriages

The Yale Law Journal article says nothing about homosexual conduct laws, though a student note published in the same journal two years later takes the position that, under the ERA, state laws prohibiting homosexual marriages would be unconstitutional.[12] The position taken by this student note was rejected by a Washington intermediate appellate court in *Singer v. Hara.*[13] Proponents of the ERA have consistently maintained that it will not invalidate laws prohibiting homosexual conduct.[14] In his testimony before the House subcommittee, Professor Emerson dealt with the issue in a single sentence: "Laws dealing with homosexual relations would likewise be unaffected, for such laws also deal with physical characteristics pertaining only to one sex."[15] This assertion notwithstanding, the attempt to bring homosexual conduct laws under the "unique physical characteristics" umbrella raises serious theoretical problems. The reason ties back to the basic rationale of the qualified absolutist standard. It permits no exceptions. In the view of its proponents, exceptions would nullify the amendment. Two qualifications, however, are recognized. And what is the difference between qualifications and exceptions? Qualifications represent circumstances in which the Equal Rights Amendment does not apply. Qualifications fall outside the amendment's reach. The classic examples are laws dealing with sperm donors and wet nurses. Those laws draw no distinctions between men and women; in the nature of things, because of physical characteristics unique to one sex, those laws are capable of applying only to one sex.

That is simply not true of laws dealing with homosexual conduct. Homosexual conduct laws involve the clearest possible kind of classification based on sex. Those laws permit Bob to marry Carol and Ted to marry Alice. But they prohibit Bob from doing what Alice may do, namely, marry Ted. Why? Solely because of his sex.

Physical characteristics unique to one sex have nothing to do with either homosexual behavior or laws prohibiting it. It is true that only members of the same sex are involved with each other in the prohibited conduct. But that fact is irrelevant. By definition, the first qualification hinges on characteristics unique to one sex. Practicing homosexuals are found among both sexes.

The argument that laws prohibiting homosexual conduct would be constitutional under the Equal Rights Amendment so long as they prohibit both relations between men and relations between women might be sufficient under a strict judicial scrutiny, compelling state interest, or similar test—but not under a qualified absolute standard. The only reason that homosexuals are forbidden to do what others are permitted to do is because of their sex.

It is true that the Washington intermediate appellate court in *Singer v. Hara* rejected an attack under that state's ERA on a Washington law prohibiting homosexual marriages.[16] But that is only one decision, by one lower state court, and the opinion fails to resolve or even consider the theoretical inconsistencies discussed above. Based on the *Singer* case and previous legislative history, Professor Emerson testified at the Senate hearings on extension of the time for ratification: "We certainly know that in view of the legislative history, the courts are not going to say that the ERA requires homosexual marriages. If you can be sure of one thing in the law, I would be sure of that."[17]

If Professor Emerson's prediction comes true it will be in spite of the rationale underlying the constitutional standard he advocates. Laws prohibiting homosexual marriages are the classic case of discrimination based on sex. Again, they prohibit men, solely because they are men, from doing what women are permitted to do: marry other men. And the proposition that such laws are based on a characteristic unique to one sex is unsupportable. Neither the *Singer* opinion nor Professor Emerson nor anyone else has ever attempted to support it with anything more solid than the bare fact of its assertion. Homosexuality and homosexual conduct are found among members of both sexes. Unless the doctrinal underpinnings of qualified absolutism are completely ignored, therefore, practicing homosexuals should be among the principal beneficiaries of the ERA.

Sexually Integrated Publicly Owned Sleeping Facilities

Under a qualified absolutist interpretation, state laws prohibiting unmarried men and women from sleeping in the same dormitory rooms of state colleges, if they choose to do so, would be unconstitutional. The same would be true of federal laws or regulations dealing with intersexual occupation of military sleeping facilities. It might be possible to preserve segregated prison cells.

Proponents of the absolute standard with qualifications attempt to bring these laws within their second qualification, which "flows from the constitutional right of privacy, established by the Supreme Court in *Griswold v. Connecticut,* 381 U.S. 479 (1965)."[18] Professor Emerson testified:

Similarly the right of privacy would permit, perhaps require, the separation of the sexes in public restrooms, segregation by sex in sleeping quarters of prisons or similar public institutions, and a certain segregation of living conditions in the Armed Forces.[19]

Segregation of sleeping quarters by sex in public institutions is clearly a classification based on sex. The state permits a woman to sleep in the same dormitory room occupied by another woman. The only reason that a man cannot sleep there is that he is a man. Since by definition the absolute standard prohibits all such distinctions, the only way to save this one is to fit it within one of the qualifications. This time the suggested candidate is the second qualification, the right of privacy.

Privacy as a constitutional value means several different things.[20] The right of privacy established by *Griswold v. Connecticut* and other cases is in essence the right of individuals to make certain decisions for themselves pertaining to their sexual lives and their family lives without governmental interference. *Griswold* held unconstitutional a Connecticut statute prohibiting the sale, dissemination, or use of contraceptives. The abortion cases, *Roe v. Wade*[21] and its progeny, relied on a similar rationale: at least during the early stages of pregnancy, the decision of whether or not to bear a child is a personal one for the woman and her doctor. She has a constitutional right, rooted in privacy considerations, to make that decision, free of governmental interference.

The *Griswold v. Connecticut* and *Roe v. Wade* line of privacy cases is not a model of internal consistency. In at least one respect, however, the cases are very consistent: they deal exclusively with the right of the individual to be free from governmental interference.

The attempt to save laws prohibiting cohabitation in public facilities apparently follows this reasoning:

1. As a constitutional principle, the Equal Rights Amendment must take its place alongside other constitutional principles and accommodate its demands with theirs.
2. One such principle is the right of privacy.
3. Sleeping patterns involve privacy, and therefore a person's privacy in these matters would be protected.

Assuming that the courts would follow this line of reasoning, it does nothing to save the constitutionality of state efforts to prevent unmarried couples from sleeping together in the college dorm or the army barracks, if that is what the couples want to do. It should save laws requiring that body searches of suspected criminals be conducted only by individuals whose sex is the same as that of the person being searched, and it should preserve the government's right to provide separate public toilet facilities. Both of these represent government efforts to assist individuals in their own efforts to preserve their privacy.

But dorms and barracks are different, at least where willing cohabitants are involved. The sole function of the *Griswold* right of privacy is to prevent governmental intrusions into individual decisions that are privacy related. For that reason it fits the body search and public toilet circumstances, where the individual wants to remain isolated from contact with members of the opposite sex. In the dormitory circumstance, the individuals are not asking government to save them from unwanted intrusions on their privacy. Quite the opposite. They want to sleep together. A no-exception interpretation of the Equal Rights Amendment entitles them to sleep together. They cannot be prevented from doing so by a government armed only with a constitutional doctrine whose exclusive office is to protect individuals from government.[22]

Segregated prison cells may be another matter. In various contexts, the courts have held that prisoners, because of their conviction for serious offenses against society, have forfeited certain rights that they would otherwise enjoy, including constitutional rights.[23] This could include rights guaranteed by the Equal Rights Amendment. Once again, however, that argument will be more difficult to sustain if the Equal Rights Amendment incorporates an absolute standard, whether qualified or not. If no exceptions means no exceptions, traditional approaches to prisoners' rights could also fall.

Even if the right of privacy would be a sufficient qualification to permit segregation by sex in sleeping quarters, it would not prevent broad integration of public student housing. That is, state colleges and universities would be required to allow male and female students to live in the same buildings, even in side-by-side bedrooms. In this sense, at least, "coed dorms" appear to be a certain result of the Equal Rights Amendment.

Two final comments are appropriate. The first is simply a repetition that the invalidation of rules dealing with segregated sleeping quarters in publicly owned institutions depends on the adoption of an absolute or qualified absolute standard. Under any other standard there is no particular basis for analysis of these issues; the most one can say is that such laws might or might not be invalid. There is a statement in the minority portion of the House report that the amendment would not alter "the traditional power of the State to regulate cohabitation and sexual activity by unmarried persons."[24] This statement appears side by side, however, with an assertion that Professor Emerson's qualified absolute standard rules the ERA.

Second, for many people in today's world, extramarital promiscuity is none of society's business, and any kind of governmental effort to stop it ought to be invalidated. For present purposes, the point is not whether these laws are good or bad. The point is that each American citizen, in making his or her decision whether the Equal Rights Amendment is in our national interest, should take its possible effects into account. For those who believe sexual promiscuity should be none of government's business, the ERA poses no threat, at least with respect to matters discussed in this section. For those who disagree, the amendment poses significant risks. If either variant of the absolutist standard is adopted, some of the risks become a virtual reality.

The Equal Rights Amendment and Family Law

Family law is the area in which it is easiest to predict probable effects of the Equal Rights Amendment. While some of the results are unclear, the fate of most laws dealing with family relations should be the same whether the courts follow an absolutist or some other standard.

The probable changes are considered under four separate headings.

Alimony, Child Support, and Custody

The general effect of the ERA on these laws will be to eliminate general presumptions favoring wives over husbands, thus requiring the courts to consider more carefully the facts of each individual case.

Most states presently have statutes imposing upon the father the obligation of support for the family.[1] Nonperformance of this obligation, as in the case of desertion or simple refusal to support, may result either in criminal penalties or civil damage actions, or both.[2] In the event of divorce, alimony obligations frequently rest more heavily on husbands than wives, either because of statutory requirements or judicial case law. This is often true even where wives in fact have greater financial resources. Statutes in some states have prohibited absolutely the imposition of alimony obligations on wives, but an Alabama law[3] to this effect was held unconstitutional under the equal protection clause of the Fourteenth Amendment in *Orr v. Orr.*[4] Consistent with the general premise that the obligation of support belongs to the husband, many state laws provide heavier child support obligation for the husband in the event of divorce.[5] With regard to custody, most laws favor the mother, at least in the case of younger children.[6] Each of these laws favors the wife or mother, and each is grounded in an apparent assumption concerning the roles of men and women.[7] One is the provider and the other the homemaker.

It is quite clear that under the Equal Rights Amendment all these laws would be unconstitutional.[8] This is not to say that the amendment would leave divorced families without the protections of alimony and support decrees. Rather, the presumptions and procedures that favor women solely because they are women and that impose obligations on men solely because they are men would no longer be valid. With respect to alimony, the courts would inquire into the actual income-producing potential of each spouse, without any presumption that the man probably would pay rather than the woman. Concerning child custody, the focus would be on whether in each particular instance the children were in fact closer to the father or the mother, and whether their welfare would be more adequately assured in the custody of one parent or the other.[9]

There is a potential short-range problem concerning alimony and child support decrees. The problem has two dimensions, the first of which is similar to the labor legislation issue considered in Chapter 10. If existing state laws are held unconstitutional—as they almost certainly will be—and if some states do not enact new legislation during the two-year period between the amendment's passage date and its effective date, might some states be left without any alimony and child support laws at all? The proponents' answer is the same as in the labor context: rather than nullifying the entire statute, the courts would hold it equally applicable to men and women.[10] In the labor legislation context, this position raises serious problems. In the alimony and child support context, it does not. The reason is that the offending provision in the alimony or child support statute is a presumption favoring one sex. The courts can solve the problem by holding that presumption unconstitutional. There is no need to rewrite the statute. Nothing more is required than to nullify the invalid portion and sever it from the valid portion.[11]

It is possible, however, that a court might find the entire alimony statute unconstitutional. In a recent New York County Supreme Court decision, the judge became impatient with the New York Legislature's slowness in redrafting the state's gender-based alimony provisions to conform with *Orr* and held the entire statute unconstitutional. This left the court without any authority to award alimony.[12]

The second dimension of this problem concerns judgments or awards that courts have already made under statutes that may subsequently be held invalid. Will these previous judgments also be held retroactively invalid? This possibility led Congressman Wiggins to state:

> I respectfully make this observation, that in the single area of
> support and the duty of support, the equal-rights amendment
> would bring a lot of real equity to the law in the future, but that
> it would subject millions of people to potential chaos concerning
> the validity of existing orders.[13]

While this concern cannot be entirely discounted, it is subject to ameliorating considerations. First, the self-interest of the parties involved would lead them to take advantage of the two-year grace period between the passage date and the effective date. Second, within the past two decades, federal courts have shown increasing willingness to make their constitutional holdings prospective only.[14] Applying the prospectivity approach in this context would mean that state alimony and support statutes favoring one sex would be held unconstitutional only insofar as future decrees were concerned.[15]

Domicile

Domicile is a concept with many important legal ramifications. Domicile refers to the legal relationship that a person has with a particular state. Every person has a domicile, and no one has more than one domicile at any one time. The state where a person is domiciled is the only state where that person may vote, run for public office, be liable for certain taxes, sue for divorce,[16] be preferred by the state university in matters of both admission and tuition, and have his or her estate administered upon death.

Traditionally the wife's domicile has been that of her husband. She has been able to establish a separate domicile only under limited circumstances.[17] Examples are where it would be hazardous to her health to continue to live in the place of her husband's domicile, or where the marriage relationship has so deteriorated that it is unrealistic to expect that the two will continue to live together, or, in some cases, where the husband has consented to her establishing a separate domicile.[18]

The Equal Rights Amendment would probably require a single, uniform rule for every state: husband and wife would have the same rights of domicile selection. One consequence would be the invalidity of present laws providing that a wife's refusal to follow her husband to a new domicile amounts to desertion or abandonment.[19] One other effect concerns the domicile of children. The traditional approach, that children take the domicile of their father,[20] would probably not survive. States would likely be free to pick any reasonable alternative, so long as it is sex neutral. That is, a state might permit children above a certain age to elect the domicile of either parent, in the event the parents have different domiciles, or the state could provide that the child would have the same domicile as the parent with whom the child spends the most time. In some cases the parents might be living together but maintain separate domiciles; for example, the home might be in Kansas City, Missouri, but with one of the parents maintaining a domicile in Kansas City, Kansas, where he or she practiced law or medicine. In such a case the domicile of the children should be in Missouri, where the home is.

Property Tax Exemptions, Business Dealings, and Community Property

Under any standard the ERA would probably invalidate tax exemptions for widows solely on the basis that they are widows. On the other hand, property tax exemptions to the surviving spouse of a deceased breadwinner would probably be held constitutional.

Historically, the laws of the various states have imposed differing disabilities on married women engaging in business transactions. Over the years the restrictions of these laws have diminished.[21] The Equal Rights Amendment under any test would accelerate this liberalizing trend, and either absolutist standard would do away with them altogether, since they fit neither of the specified qualifications.

At common law—the law that this nation inherited from England at the time of its independence—the husband not only had complete control over property that the wife brought into the marriage but he also had control over her earnings during marriage.[22] Today eight states (Arizona, California, Idaho, Louisiana, Nevada, New Mexico, Texas, and Washington) have community property systems that generally govern the property rights of husband and wife.[23] The basic concepts are that any property brought into the marriage by either spouse remains that spouse's separate property, and any earnings by either spouse during the marriage belong equally to the two of them.[24]

The community property system is generally considered more favorable to women than other systems. It recognizes that while earnings during the marriage might have been acquired by one spouse or the other, each performs functions that are valuable to the marriage, and that it is neither practical nor desirable to attempt to assess the comparative worth of these contributions. There was one prominent feature of community property laws, however, that has been sex discriminatory and probably would have been held unconstitutional under any Equal Rights Amendment standard. That feature, known as male management, has given the husband the exclusive management of community property. However, in the period from 1967 to 1980, all the community property states have adopted the concept of equal management. And most of this change has occurred since the ERA was passed by Congress in March of 1972. As of that time only Texas (in 1967) and Washington (in 1972) had adopted the equal management concept.[25]

Name Changes

The Yale Law Journal article asserts: "The Equal Rights Amendment would not permit a legal requirement, or even a legal presumption, that a woman takes her husband's name at the time of marriage.... A man and woman would still be free to adopt the same name, and most couples would probably do so for reasons of identification, social custom, personal preference, or consistency in naming children. Howver, the legal barriers would have been removed for a woman who wanted to use the name that was not her husband's."[26]

The legislative history contains surprisingly little discussion concerning this issue, aside from Senator Ervin's excoriating remarks in his dissent from the Senate report.[27]

The safest prediction that can be made is that if the qualified absolutist test advocated by Professor Emerson and the other authors of the Yale Law Journal article is adopted, then their statement concerning the fate of name change laws will likely come to pass. Obviously, the requirement that the wife take her husband's name involves a sex classification and it has nothing to do with physical characteristics unique to one sex or the right of privacy.

If something short of a qualified absolutist standard is adopted, then prediction becomes more difficult. Under a nonabsolutist standard, name change laws should be left in place because of the confusion that would otherwise exist.[28] The Yale Law Journal authors contend that states should be free to require that couples adopt the same name, so long as they are not required to take either the husband's name or the wife's name.[29] This, of course, is consistent with the overall absolutist approach that no sex classifications are to be permitted. But the gains in important personal liberties from such a rule are so far outweighed by the resulting confusions that under anything other than an absolutist standard, I believe that state name change laws would have a good chance of surviving.

The Equal Rights Amendment, Labor, and Education

Labor Laws: "Protective" and "Restrictive"— Extension and Nullification

The labor legislation issue is really several different issues. The reason is that state labor laws that might be affected by the Equal Rights Amendment fall into several categories. Some state laws prohibit women from working at all in certain types of employment. Probably the most notorious historical examples have been laws against women working in mines and in bars. Some laws prevent women from working in jobs requiring the lifting of weights in excess of designated amounts. Others prohibit women from working at night, or for more than a maximum number of hours in a specified period.

There is another category of laws whose apparent purpose is to "protect" women. These include such benefits as minimum wages, rest periods, mandatory provision of chairs for use during rest periods, or a day of rest.

All of these laws treat women differently than men and are therefore potential victims of the Equal Rights Amendment. Not only is there disagreement concerning which of these laws would fall if the ERA were adopted; there is also disagreement as to whether invalidation would be a good thing.

One of the ERA proponents, Congressman Kastenmeier, said that the argument that " 'The amendment will wipe out existing protections for women workers' . . . seems to be the most powerful argument against the proposed amendment."[1] The "protections" to which he referred were apparently such laws as those providing for minimum wages, rest periods, and the like. The argument against their constitutionality under the Equal Rights Amendment would be that since they apply only to women they are a sex-based classification and are therefore unconstitutional.

On the theoretical level, the proponents' solution to this problem is simple and straightforward: "restrictive" discriminatory labor laws, such as "those which bar women entirely from certain occupations will be invalid."[2] Those conferring a "benefit," on the other hand, such as minimum wage laws or health and safety protections, will be extended to cover men as well as women, thereby eliminating the discrimination.[3]

Assuming that the courts agree with this proposition that beneficial laws are to be extended while restrictive laws are to be invalidated, and assuming further that a means can be devised to determine which is which, how will the beneficial laws be extended? The cleanest way would be for each state legislature to change its own laws, extending the benefits of protective labor legislation to both sexes. The Senate report points out that "the purpose of delaying the effective date of the Equal Rights Amendment for two years after ratification is to allow legislatures—particularly those which meet only in alternate years—and agencies an opportunity to review and revise their laws and regulations."[4] Experience with legislatures and how they function teaches, however, that in some instances the legislatures will not change their statutes extending the benefits to men. Does this mean that the benefits are also lost to women? This possibility is the major reason that many people, including some labor leaders,[5] have opposed the Equal Rights Amendment.

In the proponents' view, if the state legislatures do not extend the benefits of protective labor legislation to men, then the Equal Rights Amendment will. The very force of its prohibition against sex discrimination will extend the benefits of protective labor legislation to members of both sexes.[6]

There are two potential problems with this theory of invalidation of restrictions and extension of benefits. First, it is far from established that this would be an acceptable judicial procedure. Courts have frequently observed that a first-line judicial responsibility is to give effect to legislative intent.[7] It is difficult to impute to a legislature that gave protections only to members of one sex a probable intent that the benefits should be broadened to include members of both sexes if the single-sex protection were held unconstitutional. Such an approach smacks of judicial usurpation of the legislative function. It is possible that courts faced with such an option would follow the course that is more judicial in nature and simply invalidate the statute as it is written. This would leave to the legislature the policy choice of either rewriting the legislation to extend to both sexes or leaving it applicable to neither.[8]

There is an even more serious problem. The proponents' approach is to invalidate the restrictive laws and extend protective ones. But even if a court were willing to overlook the obvious legislative aspects of that task and go ahead with it, how would such a court make the critical distinction between restrictive laws and protective laws? Consider a few examples.

What about limitations on the number of hours that women can work in a day or a week? This was a major battle in earlier decades, and *Muller v. Oregon* was regarded as a watershed victory for women.[9] Was it a victory? The only fair answer is that maximum working hours for women are a benefit to some women and a restriction to others. Some women, like some men, are capable of working longer hours and prefer to work longer hours because it does them no harm and they want the money. Moreover, limiting the hours that a woman can work also limits her opportunity for overtime wages and perhaps advancement.[10]

The difficulty of drawing any meaningful categorical distinctions between restrictive and protective laws applies to every conceivable category of labor legislation. Laws barring women from certain kinds of employment have been vigorously attacked as the paradigm of restrictive laws. And yet Dr. Margaret Mead, one of this century's foremost anthropologists, sees laws getting women out of the mines as a great victory: "In the beginning of mining, there were women down those mines and children. . . . We got the women and children out of the mines you know."[11]

What about minimum wage laws for women? Are they not a clear example of protective labor legislation? Not necessarily. In some cases, minimum wage laws in fact benefit the worker. In other cases, the economic effect of minimum wage laws is not to protect the worker, and the effect of minimum wages for women is not to protect the female worker. The principal beneficiaries of minimum wage laws are the more highly skilled workers, and those who benefit most clearly from minimum wage laws for women are the more highly skilled female workers. For less skilled persons, men or women, the effect of minimum wage laws may be unemployment because such laws prohibit the employment of persons whose labor is worth less than the minimum wage. Sometimes the only advantage that the marginal, unskilled worker has is his or her willingness to work for less money. Minimum wage laws take away that advantage. Recall that in *Adkins v. Children's Hospital*[12] one of the plaintiffs attacking the District of Columbia's minimum wage law was a woman who lost her job because she was not worth the minimum wage to her employer.

What would be the effect, then, on protective labor legislation for women if the Equal Rights Amendment becomes law? Actually there are two answers to that question. The first is that a confident, definitive answer is impossible. At the very least there is substantial risk that some laws passed for the ostensible purpose of helping women in the labor market will be declared unconstitutional. If this happens it will benefit some women and disadvantage others.

The more important conclusion concerning labor legislation, protective and otherwise, is that most of the problems are being handled—and were being handled at the time of the ERA debates—by legislation, principally Title VII of the Civil Rights Act of 1964.[13] The basic thrust of Title VII is the elimination of discrimination, including sex discrimination, in matters of employment. Title VII has a broader reach than the Equal Rights Amendment in that it affects not only governmental but also private employers. Because it is federal legislation, it preempts state law where the two conflict[14] and in this respect is analogous to a constitutional provision. The major difference is that it is easier to change in the event that mistakes are discovered.

Given the basic thrust of Title VII, to eliminate distinctions between men and women in employment, most of the "protective" state laws have been invalidated.[15] At the time of the ERA hearings, this development was already in process. As observed by Dr. Bernice Sandler of the Women's Equity Action League:

> Title VII is invalidating protective legislation in case after case. Regardless of whether the equal rights amendment is passed or whether it is not passed, protective legislation is on the way out.[16]

Similarly, the Citizens' Advisory Council on the Status of Women predicted: "There will probably not be any of the prohibitory laws in effect by the time the Equal Rights Amendment is ratified, as a result of Title VII of the Civil Rights Act of 1964."[17]

The ERA and Education: Single-Sex Schools and Interscholastic Athletic Programs

The legislative history says very little about the ERA's potential effect on public schools. However, several effects could be significant, particularly if an absolutist or qualified-absolutist standard were applied. Two of these include the single-sex public school and participation in and financial support of interscholastic athletic programs.

Single-Sex Schools. The schools most obviously affected would be public schools[18] and schools covered by Congress's exercise of lawmaking authority granted by Section 2 of the Equal Rights Amendment.[19] For reasons other than constitutional requirements, single-sex schools are becoming less common, but in some parts of the country, for some purposes, school authorities still prefer them. Under the Fourteenth Amendment, the Supreme Court has narrowly upheld single-sex public schools. In *Vorchheimer v. School District,*[20] the Supreme Court affirmed by an equally divided vote[21] a decision by the United States Court of Appeals for the Third Circuit upholding a Philadelphia School Board policy of operating sex-segregated high schools for the academically gifted.[22] Given the closeness of the *Vorchheimer* decision and the general principle that an addition to an existing body of law expands the existing law, it is quite clear that, under any standard, the

Equal Rights Amendment would take away from state and local school authorities the option to decide whether in some cases all-male or all-female public schools best suit their needs.

Interscholastic Athletics: Participation and Funding. Two of the more obvious issues pertaining to interscholastic athletics are the maintenance of all-male or all-female athletic teams and the discretion of school officials to spend more on male athletic programs than on female.

In *Darrin v. Gould,*[23] discussed in Chapter 6, the Washington State Supreme Court held that, under its Equal Rights Amendment, two sisters were constitutionally entitled to participate as members of the boys' high school football team. The concurring justice agreed with the decision "with some qualms . . . exclusively upon the basis that the result is dictated by the broad and mandatory language of [the Washington ERA]."

The Washington State Supreme Court, in *Darrin v. Gould,* held that the applicable standard was something beyond strict judicial scrutiny.[24] The result is clearly dictated by an absolutist standard, and almost certainly by a qualified absolutist standard. While it is probably true that most boys are stronger than most girls, exclusion of girls from participating in boys' contact sports has nothing to do with the unique physical characteristics qualification, as narrowly defined by the advocates of the qualified absolutist standard. That qualification applies only to characteristics unique to members of one sex, and it is beyond doubt that strength and athletic ability are not unique to males. Some girls are stronger and are better athletes than some boys.

The privacy qualification would also be inapplicable in most if not all cases because, as discussed in Chapter 8, there is no *governmental* invasion of privacy against the will of the participants. The would-be athletes want to participate and raise no privacy objection. One possible privacy-related argument, however, might be the privacy interests of members of the dominant sex on the athletic teams (in the typical case, males) who object to intersexual participation in contact sports.

At least in the great majority of instances, it would seem that, under an absolutist or qualified-absolutist standard, *Darrin v. Gould* is a fair indication of what might be expected throughout the country under a national Equal Rights Amendment.[25]

Equally interesting problems would be presented by boys who want to participate on girls' athletic teams. If it is true that most boys are better athletes than most girls, the result could be the deterioration—and in some cases elimination—of girls' leagues and girls' opportunities for competitive participation. As observed by Professor Stanmeyer of the Indiana University Law School:

An Illinois Court has already decided that equality cuts both ways, and has ruled that when a school provides no participation for one sex [in a] noncontact sport, members of that sex have the right to compete for places on a girls' bowling team and boys won four out of five places on the Dixon High School team that later won the girls' State championship bowling tournament; to the disgust of adult onlookers.[26]

The validity of spending different amounts of money for men's and women's athletic programs is already at issue under existing law. The greatest potential impact is at the college level. The basic argument in favor of differential treatment is that men's athletic programs produce more revenues for the school, and it is necessary to spend more money on men's programs in order to assure their continuing revenue-producing potential. One issue under the present complex of constitutional, statutory, and administrative law is whether financial support of men's and women's programs must be equal.[27] A second issue— assuming equality is required—is how to measure the school's compliance, whether payments to each program must be equal, or whether the number of participants may be taken into account.[28] To date, there have been no definitive pronouncements on either of these issues.[29] At the very least, the Equal Rights Amendment would diminish the discretion of public school officials to spend more on one program than another. Under either of the absolutist standards, any difference in financial support would be unconstitutional. Whatever the economic justifications for such differences, they cannot be brought under either the unique physical characteristics or the privacy qualification to the absolutist standard.

11

Should ERA Become
Part of the Constitution?

The decade of the 1970s witnessed intense national debate over whether the Equal Rights Amendment is in our interest. The central feature of the debate has been confident but conflicting assertions by both sides concerning the effects of the ERA if it becomes part of the Constitution. All the congressional testimony and reports favoring the Equal Rights Amendment assert that it would not invalidate laws prohibiting homosexual relations, intersexual occupancy of sleeping facilities in public institutions, or forcible rape. Opponents of the amendment are equally convinced that these results would occur. Concerning the mandatory use of women in combat, even the proponents are in disagreement.

Both sides in this debate have missed the point. Neither during the present preratification period nor, if ratified, for decades after can anyone on this planet know what the ERA will mean. The most important question is the standard of judicial review: judicial scrutiny, strict judicial scrutiny, qualified absolutism, or something else. No one knows what that standard will be. My own best judgment is that it will be either a strict judicial scrutiny or qualified absolutist approach, which would move the standard from point A on the continuum (Diagram F) to either point B or point C. A solid argument can be made, however, for moving it all the way to point D.

Moreover, even after the standard is identified, uncertainties will still exist. The qualified absolutists contend that laws prohibiting forcible rape, homosexual conduct, and coeducational dormitories for single people will be saved by their two qualifications. I am equally convinced that laws prohibiting homosexual conduct and coeducational dorms are inconsistent with that standard. The only hope for those laws would be to persuade the courts either to adopt something other than an absolutist approach or to ignore the doctrinal underpinnings of absolutism. In the face of that kind of uncertainty, how is the conscientious citizen to make a choice?

For a few people, the answer will be easy because there are no horribles in the parade. Constitutional legalization of homosexual conduct

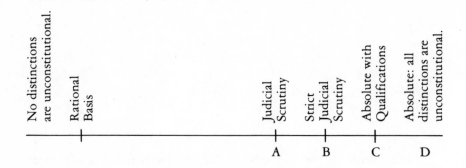

Diagram F

and coed dorms is exactly what they would like. For most people, however, these would be unwanted results and would therefore cause
serious concern. For these people the starting point for determining
whether the ERA is in our national interest is a frank recognition that
no one knows what it will mean, and no one can know what it will
mean until after it becomes part of the Constitution.

The only rational approach to the Equal Rights Amendment issue, therefore, is to recognize the risks that flow from the fact that the
amendment might be interpreted in certain ways, and then to ask
whether the benefits from the amendment outweigh those risks.

The risk side of the analysis has been the subject of preceding
chapters: the different interpretations that might be placed on the
amendment, and the comparative likelihood that one interpretation or
another might be adopted.

The analysis turns now to the benefit side: how badly is the
amendment needed and, to whatever extent the need exists, are there
better ways to satisfy it?

The Lessons of History

The perspective of history offers a helpful starting point. In 1923,
when the Equal Rights Amendment was first introduced, the Supreme
Court of the United States had never even dealt with the argument
that laws discriminating against women violate constitutional guarantees of equality. Highly offensive sex discriminatory practices had been
consistently upheld.[1] Furthermore, women had enjoyed the most fundamental of all political rights—the right to vote—for only three years.

Three decades later, in the 1950s, a modified version of the ERA
passed the Senate twice, but proponents characterized the modifications

as an effective nullification.[2] As of that time, an equal protection argument had at least been presented to the U.S. Supreme Court in a sex discrimination case, but the Court easily rejected it and upheld the discrimination.[3]

Passage of the amendment by Congress in 1972 was preceded by almost two years of congressional consideration. Throughout most of those two years—more than a century after the general guarantee of "equal protection of the law" had been written into the Fourteenth Amendment—the equal protection clause had never been used to invalidate a sex discriminatory law. And most of the ERA proponents despaired of ever obtaining equality for women through the Fourteenth Amendment. Nevertheless, many of them conceded that, if the Supreme Court were to apply the Fourteenth Amendment's equal protection clause to women, the Equal Rights Amendment would be unnecessary.[4] Others disagreed.[5]

Reed v. Reed, the first Supreme Court case to hold a gender-based classification unconstitutional under the Fourteenth Amendment, was handed down in November 1971, after the House of Representatives had passed the Equal Rights Amendment but before Senate passage.[6] As is usually the case with developing constitutional doctrines, it was impossible to forecast in late 1971 how much protection *Reed v. Reed* would actually afford against sex discrimination. Specifically, the unanswered question was whether the rational basis standard would apply, so that invalidation of gender-based discriminations would be rare, or whether sex discrimination would be treated the same as racial discrimination, subject to strict judicial scrutiny.

Over the intervening decade since *Reed v. Reed,* the Supreme Court has developed a rather comprehensive body of case law dealing with sex discrimination. The standard is neither rational basis nor strict judicial scrutiny. It lies somewhere between the two. The result has been that the number of cases upheld and the number invalidated have been about equal. Whether the Supreme Court has gone too far, not far enough, or just about as far as it should is a matter for individual decision.[7]

But it is beyond dispute that the big leap has already been made. One of the proper roles for a constitutional amendment in achieving reform is to make large changes, to reach new ground previously unexplored. With respect to sex discrimination, a change of that magnitude was needed in 1971. It had been needed for decades and even centuries prior to 1971, but nothing had happened. Today, the situation is very different. There is no longer any question whether equality is constitutionally guaranteed to women. It is.

Some may argue that the principal reason for this change has been the pendency of the Equal Rights Amendment. That may or may not be true. In any event, it is largely irrelevant. Whatever the reason for our movement from nothing to judicial scrutiny along the sexual equality continuum, the fact is that we are there.

Massive Change or Flexibility?

Regardless of what the issues might have been in the 1920s when the amendment was first introduced, in the 1950s when it passed the Senate, or in the early 1970s when it was formally proposed by Congress, the central issues concerning the need for an Equal Rights Amendment in the 1980s are:

1. Whether the greater need is another radical, massive change in the constitutional rules dealing with distinctions between men and women, or

2. Whether the greater need is for flexibility in determining what kinds of distinctions between men and women are really in our national interest, and what kinds are not.

This correctly characterizes the issues today for this reason: the only room left for a change so great as to warrant a constitutional amendment is a change to an absolutist standard, qualified or otherwise. If the Equal Rights Amendment does nothing more than move us along the continuum from judicial scrutiny to strict judicial scrutiny, then the change is not worthy of a constitutional amendment. It is certainly not worth the risk of more radical change.

The real issue for each citizen, therefore, is whether he or she feels that all—or nearly all—governmental distinctions between men and women should be constitutionally eliminated. It is clear that some people would answer this question yes. But the great majority probably would answer it no. Almost none of those who testified at the congressional hearings, or those who drafted the reports recommending congressional passage, intended such an extreme result. They did not want to do away with virtually all governmental distinctions between men and women. They wanted a constitutional guarantee of equality for women. At the time there was none. Today there is.

For those Americans who share the view that we should leave some flexibility to make some governmental distinctions between men and women, another constitutional amendment is not the answer.

The second major purpose asserted by the proponents in urging congressional passage of the ERA was that such an amendment was needed as a symbol.[8] It is true that constitutional amendments can serve as symbols. The question is, a symbol of what? More specifically, how firmly should we freeze the capacity of our governmental structure to react? If we now have all or substantially all the answers concerning the distinctions that government should be able to make between men and women—particularly if we are convinced that there should be none or very few—then a constitutional amendment is an appropriate symbol.

For a constitutional amendment is the surest way to prevent government from drawing distinctions. If, on the other hand, we are still at the stage where we need to feel our way, committed to equality in the large matters like employment and promotion opportunity, educational opportunity, political activity, and equal pay for equal work, but still uncertain about such things as the draft, combat, and promiscuity in state college dormitories, then a constitutional amendment is the worst possible choice of a symbol.[9]

Experience Indicates the Need for Flexibility

Many people have the perception that, within the last few years, appointments to federal and state judgeships and to important executive positions in government have favored women. That is, if the appointee had not been a woman, someone else more qualified would have been appointed. Some believe that such preferences are not only fair and appropriate but necessary. They compensate for past discriminations against women and provide highly visible role models for future generations. Others take the view that whatever mistakes may have been made in the past, the burden of the corrective should not rest upon persons in today's society who have done no wrong.

The important issue is not whether the perception is correct, nor which side in the debate is right. The real issue is the debate itself. It should continue. In some instances treating women better than men with respect to government appointments is probably a good idea, and in other instances it is not. Moreover, whatever the balance of relevant considerations today, whether in general or in specific cases, the balance probably will be different a generation from now. Neither for this generation nor for those that will follow is it in our national interest to cut off debate on that issue by making unconstitutional government's power to prefer women.

Regardless of where we were ten years ago, or thirty years ago, or a hundred years ago, today we are at the fine-tuning stage. The need is for careful case-by-case examination of whether and to what extent men and women should be treated differently. A constitutional amendment, very simply, is not a fine-tuning instrument. It has more the qualities of a sledgehammer.

An incident that occurred during the period of my service in the United States Department of Justice illustrates the degrees of flexibility of different sources of law. A federal statute prohibiting sex discrimination by schools receiving federal financial assistance provides, among other things, that its provisions shall not be interpreted to prohibit father-son or mother-daughter activities as long as there is reasonably comparable opportunity for each.[10] In 1976 some administrators at the Department of Health, Education, and Welfare decided that a certain school district was not in compliance and determined to prevent further father-son banquets in that district until corrective steps were taken. The plan was never implemented—indeed, knowledge of its existence was limited—because some senior officials at the White House heard about it and brought it to an end with a telephone call.

The White House officials who reversed it considered the short-lived ban on father-son school banquets a silly decision. The reality is that in a government administered by human beings, we have to accept the fact that from time to time there will be silly decisions. The judiciary is also inhabited by human beings and they are not immune from the same kinds of mistakes that other human beings make. In the case of the father-son banquet decision, the mistake was easily correctible, requiring nothing more than a simple telephone call. If the same result had been unambiguously written into the statute, the corrective would have been more difficult, requiring congressional action. But by far the most inflexible source of law is a judicial decision interpreting a constitutional provision. Mistakes at that level can be corrected only by the death, retirement, or change of mind of Supreme Court justices, or by a constitutional amendment. The likelihood of any of these is extraordinarily rare. Over the history of our republic, literally thousands of constitutional amendments have been proposed. Excluding the Bill of Rights, whose adoption was part of the commitment for ratification of the Constitution,[11] only sixteen have been adopted.

Perhaps the best evidence that we are closer to the fine-tuning stage than to the major overhaul stage is provided by the 1980 experience with the draft. One of the few ERA results on which everyone agrees is that, if the amendment passes, women must be subject to the draft whenever men are. When the reinstitution of compulsory military service became an issue in 1980, the companion question was whether women should be subject to it. Most of the resistance was to drafting anyone, but a separate issue was equally identifiable and almost as strong: if there is a draft, should women be included? Leaders of several groups supporting the Equal Rights Amendment spoke in favor of equal treatment.[12] But our national legislators—who usually are a fair bellwether of national public opinion—separated the issues fairly early in the debate and determined that even if compulsory military service were to be reestablished, it would not apply to women.[13] Under the ERA Congress would not have had that choice.

Even as to one of the few ERA consequences on which everyone agrees, therefore, the 1980 draft experience shows that our nation is not at a point of consensus. We are not ready to harden the decision process into constitutional concrete. We need the leeway to make decisions on a case-by-case basis as particular issues—the draft among them—arise at different times and under different circumstances. Obviously this will not be done in a constitutional vacuum. Always in the background is the Fourteenth Amendment's guarantee that gender-based discrimination will be subject to judicial scrutiny.

Of course there are still examples of unfair sexual discrimination. Of course changes need to be made. But they should be made with a scalpel, not an axe. The tools for that kind of change are available. Indeed, changes by scalpel are already at work through the whole spectrum of law, including constitutional guarantees, statutes, administrative regulations, and ample authority to enact more statutes or administrative regulations as they are needed.

Adequate legislative authority exists without an additional constitutional amendment. Other things being equal—particularly if the subject matter does not require national uniformity—the best unit of government to enact laws is the smallest unit that has authority to do so. State and local governments have far-reaching powers, generally called police powers, to act in the interest of the general welfare of the people.[14] Accordingly they would have power to enact any conceivably necessary law. This is demonstrated by the liberalization that has occurred in state laws during the decade of the 1970s dealing with such subjects as family law (particularly the "tender years" doctrine and the circumstances under which a wife may establish a separate domicile), and the adoption of the equal management concept in community property states.[15]

In some instances, national uniformity might be preferred. While Congress's powers do not reach as many subjects as the states' police powers,[16] congressional enactments of Title VII of the Civil Rights Act and the Equal Pay Act[17] demonstrate that, under existing constitutional authorization, Congress too can be a significant force in making changes where changes are needed.

Shifts in Governmental Power

There is another cost of the Equal Rights Amendment. It is a cost that is necessarily involved in any constitutional amendment limiting what government can do, and particularly what state government can do. The cost involves shifts in governmental power. In the case of the Equal Rights Amendment, the shifts would occur along two planes.

By definition, a constitutional amendment which limits what government can do places its limitations on the legislature, within whose policymaking domain the power would otherwise fall. And since the interpretation of constitutional amendments is a judicial function, the decrease in legislative power is accompanied by an increase in judicial power. For example, if the Equal Rights Amendment were determined to prohibit separation of the sexes in college dormitories, the courts would make that determination by interpreting the amendment. The effect would be that the authority to decide this policy issue would shift from the legislature to the courts.

Most of the laws that would be held unconstitutional under the ERA are state laws. Accordingly, governmental power would shift not only from the legislature to the judiciary, but also from the smaller governmental unit (the state) to the larger (the federal government).[18]

Even in the absence of constitutional adjudication, there would probably be a legislative power shift from the states to the federal government, increasing the policymaking power of Congress and decreasing that of the state legislatures. It is a shift that would be accomplished as a result of Section 2 of the amendment. Before 1971 the proposed Equal Rights Amendment vested legislative enforcement authority jointly in Congress and the states. In 1971 state legislative enforcement authority was eliminated in favor of the present language of Section 2, which states: "Congress shall have power to enforce, by appropriate legislation, the provisions of this Article."

There is little doubt that Section 2 would shift legislative power from the states to the Congress. This would occur even if Section 2 were interpreted, as some of the proponents contend, not to have affirmatively constricted state powers in this area.[19] The constriction would necessarily result from expanded federal authority. The federal government, unlike the states, is a government of specific, enumerated powers, which means that anything the federal government does must be authorized by some constitutional provision. Within the sphere of its constitutionally authorized powers, however, the supremacy clause of the Constitution, contained in Article VI, provides that federal authority is supreme; that is, federal authority takes precedence where federal and state authority conflict. Accordingly, expanding the constitutional bases for congressional action in any area necessarily causes a corresponding reduction of the powers of state governments once Congress exercises its newly created constitutional power.[20]

In the case of some constitutional amendments, shifts of governmental power represent costs that are worth paying in order to secure the constitutional guarantee. And some people feel that governmental power shifts from the legislature to the judiciary,[21] or from state and local governments to the national government, are desirable. The only point is this: for those who believe that, other things being equal, it is better to vest governmental power in smaller units rather than larger, and in elected legislators who must periodically answer to the people than in nonelected judges, the shifts in governmental power that would accompany the Equal Rights Amendment represent another significant cost.

The Fourteenth Amendment Analogy

The potential dangers of the Equal Rights Amendment are posed by its breadth, its vagueness, and its uncertainty. No one knows how many specific prohibitions are included or are not included within its broad, unqualified declaration that there shall be no governmental distinctions on account of sex. But vagueness is also a characteristic of the Fourteenth Amendment, on whose existence a substantial part of the argument against the Equal Rights Amendment is based. Is it not unfair and inconsistent, therefore, to build an argument against the ERA on the combination of criticizing the vagueness of the proposed amendment while at the same time proclaiming the adequacy of the equal protection clause of the Fourteenth Amendment?

For anyone willing to learn the lessons of history, experience with the Fourteenth Amendment provides one of the most persuasive lessons why the Equal Rights Amendment should not be adopted. It is true that the Fourteenth Amendment, like the proposed Twenty-seventh, is vague. Look what the courts have done with that vagueness. At one period of our nation's history they used it to invalidate a broad spectrum of state laws regulating businesses,[22] including laws designed to protect the health of men and women in high health-risk employments. In more recent times the same amendment has been used, and is still being used, to prevent states from prohibiting or regulating abortions.[23] Many people thought that the Court's substantive due process nullification of governmental economic regulations was a good idea. Many people also agree with the Court's abortion decisions. The present point is not whether these decisions are good or bad. The point is that anyone who thinks that a constitutional amendment with the vagueness of the Fourteenth or the proposed Twenty-seventh is not an open invitation, and indeed directive, to perpetual judicial policymaking, is not aware of what the Supreme Court has been doing since about the 1890s.[24]

Does this mean that the Fourteenth Amendment should never have been adopted? Not at all. The Fourteenth Amendment brought about comprehensive changes that were needed. They were changes that only a constitutional amendment could achieve. Before the Fourteenth Amendment the guarantees of the Bill of Rights were not binding on the states. Aside from the guarantee of jury trial and the prohibition against ex post facto laws, state governments were not obligated to follow any standards of fairness in state criminal proceedings. Due process of law was binding on the federal government, but not the states. Most important for present purposes, there was no constitutional guarantee of equality anywhere in the Constitution.

The existence and history of the Fourteenth Amendment are relevant to the Equal Rights Amendment for three reasons. First, given the fact that the Constitution contained no guarantee of equality prior to the Fourteenth Amendment, the vagueness risk was worth taking. Now that there is a general guarantee of equality which extends to all groups, including women, the analysis is different. The vagueness risks are the same; the need is not. With the Fourteenth Amendment's guarantee of equality extending to all people, it is difficult to make a case for a separate guarantee of equality applicable to any group already covered by the equal protection clause. And if one particular group were to be singled out for such special treatment, it is hard to make the case that it should be a group that is not, in fact, a minority.

Second, the Fourteenth Amendment teaches that the risks of constitutional vagueness are never-ending. Vague amendments constitute a continuing, open-ended invitation to any new generation of federal judges to fill their ample vessels with new doctrine. The Fourteenth Amendment is particularly instructive in this regard. The first radical venture into judicial policymaking (when judges substituted their judgment for that of the legislature in government regulation of business) did not begin until almost thirty years after the amendment had become part of the Constitution.[25] It was a venture that lasted four decades and which, within its particular substantive sphere (economic regulation), today lies largely dormant.[26] Thirty years later the process started again, and it is continuing, this time affecting such substantive matters as contraceptives and abortions. The subject matter is different, but the process is not. Neither is the constitutional amendment under whose banner the process occurs.

The third lesson of the Fourteenth Amendment experience concerns the difficulty of undoing mistakes once they occur. During the economic-regulation round of the Supreme Court's fascination with substantive due process, the correction took forty years. For the abortion round, the correction has not yet occurred. Maybe it never will.[27]

In the case of the Fourteenth Amendment, the risks were worth running because the need for massive change was great. The changes were achieved, and the risks have proven to be real. But the risks entailed in the proposed Twenty-seventh Amendment are not worth running because the need for massive change is not great. Indeed, massive change is the biggest risk.

A

Appendix
Supreme Court Cases
Dealing with Sex Discrimination, 1971–80

Sex discrimination during the last decade has been one of the most prolific areas of constitutional adjudication. The landmark cases establishing gender as a classification subject to judicial scrutiny by the Court are discussed in Chapter 4. *Reed v. Reed,* 404 U.S. 71 (1971); *Frontiero v. Richardson,* 411 U.S. 677 (1973); *Craig v. Boren,* 429 U.S. 190 (1976). Many other questions concerning sex discrimination have come before the Court since 1971. The result has been relatively balanced, with the Court upholding gender classifications in several instances and invalidating them in several others. Following is (A) a list of cases in which the classification has been invalidated; (B) a list of cases in which the classification has been upheld; and brief discussions of cases dealing with (C) pregnancy, (D) abortion, and (E) Title VII of the Civil Rights Act of 1964.

A. Cases Invalidating Gender-Based Classifications

1. *Stanton v. Stanton,* 421 U.S. 7 (1975). The Court invalidated a Utah statute which placed the age of majority for females at eighteen and for males at twenty-one, declaring that old notions about men and women are not sufficient justification for gender-based classification. Some of the old notions that are no longer valid include: (1) the man's primary responsibility is to provide a home and its essentials; (2) a man's obtaining an education or training before undertaking to provide a home is salutary; (3) girls tend to mature faster than boys; and (4) girls tend to marry earlier than boys.

2. *Taylor v. Louisiana,* 419 U.S. 522 (1975). The Court invalidated a jury-selection scheme virtually identical to the one upheld fourteen years earlier in *Hoyt v. Florida.*[1] *Taylor* was not decided as an equal protection case but on the grounds that the jury-selection scheme abridged the defendant's Sixth Amendment right to a trial by an impartial jury, a right pertaining to the states as well as the federal government by application of the due process clause of the Fourteenth Amendment.

3. *Weinberger v. Wiesenfeld,* 420 U.S. 636 (1975). The Court invalidated a provision of the Federal Social Security Act providing survivor's benefits to widows but not to widowers. The case was brought by a young widower whose wage-earning wife had died giving birth to their son. The Court granted the benefits to the widower, declaring that the law violates the due process clause of the Fifth Amendment[2] because it unjustifiably discriminates against

female wage earners by affording less protection for their survivors. Laws will not be upheld which are based on the twin assumptions: (1) man's primary place is at work, woman's at home; and (2) women who do work are secondary breadwinners whose employment is less valuable to the family than the employment of the man of the family.

4. *Califano v. Goldfarb*, 430 U.S. 199 (1977). The Court nullified a social security provision qualifying a widow for survivor's benefits automatically but allowing such benefits to a widower only upon proof that his wife supplied at least three-fourths of the couple's support (all of her own and at least half of his). A plurality opinion followed the pattern established in *Wiesenfeld*, stating that the provision unjustifiably discriminates against women as breadwinners. Justice Stevens, however, who cast the deciding vote, viewed it as discrimination against the surviving male spouse with no justification other than it was "merely the accidental byproduct of [the legislators'] traditional way of thinking about females."[3]

5. *Caban v. Mohammed*, 441 U.S. 380 (1979). The Court nullified a New York law permitting unwed mothers but not unwed fathers to block the adoption of their children by withholding consent. The Court held that although the state's interest in providing for the well-being of illegitimate children is an important one, the law bears no substantial relation to this interest.[4] The opinion stated that the underlying generalizations concerning parental roles are not sufficient to support gender-based distinctions. The dissent emphasized that this holding is not retroactive and is narrowly limited to similar fact situations. Compare this case with *Parham v. Hughes*, pp. 94–95 *infra*, in which the Court upheld a distinction between mothers of illegitimate children and fathers of illegitimate children.

6. *Davis v. Passman*, 442 U.S. 228 (1979). The Court held that a person whose Fourteenth Amendment right to equal protection has been violated has the right to sue for damages. Congressman Otto Passman fired his deputy administrative assistant Shirley Davis because he had concluded "that it was essential that the understudy to my Administrative Assistant be a man."[5] The lower court did not determine whether Ms. Davis's equal protection rights had been violated. It held that even if her rights had been violated, she could not sue to collect damages from her former boss. In other words, the right to equal protection does not carry with it the right to collect damages for a violation of that constitutional guarantee. The Supreme Court reversed this decision and held that a victim of sex discrimination in violation of the Fifth Amendment[6] has the right to sue for damages. The Supreme Court remanded the case back to the lower court for a trial of the merits of the case; that is, to determine whether Ms. Davis's Fifth Amendment rights were indeed violated and, if so, to what damages she was entitled. Another issue left to be decided by the lower court was: to what degree was the congressman shielded from suit by the speech or debate clause of the Constitution?[7] These issues were never decided, however, because the case was subsequently settled out of court.

7. *Orr v. Orr*, 440 U.S. 268 (1979). The Court invalidated an Alabama statute permitting divorce decrees to impose alimony obligations on divorced husbands but not divorced wives, regardless of their comparative financial circumstances. Lillian Orr sought to have her former husband adjudged in con-

tempt of court for failure to pay the alimony previously awarded to her. The Court held that the state's preference for the allocation of family responsibilities, under which the husband is the provider and the wife a dependent, is not sufficient to justify the gender-based classification. Females "are not destined solely for the home" and males solely "for the marketplace and world of ideas."[8] The Court also held that the statute's gender-based classification was not substantially related to the alleged objectives of (1) providing for needy spouses or (2) compensating women for past discrimination during marriage.

8. *Califano v. Westcott*, 433 U.S. 76 (1979). The Court nullified a social security provision granting benefits to dependent children when the father becomes unemployed but not when the mother becomes unemployed. The Court held that the gender-based classification was not related to any important statutory goals but was just "part of the 'baggage of sexual stereotypes' that presumes that the father has the primary responsibility to provide" for the family.[9]

9. *Wengler v. Druggists Mutual Insurance Co.*, 100 S.Ct. 1540 (1980). The Court invalidated a Missouri worker's compensation statute requiring a widower, upon the work-related death of his wife, to prove incapacity or dependence before he could receive death benefits; widows had no such requirements. The administrative efficiency of presuming that women are generally dependent on male wage earners was not sufficient to justify the discrimination.

B. Cases Upholding Gender-Based Classifications

1. *Kahn v. Shevin*, 416 U.S. 351 (1974). The Court upheld a Florida statute which grants widows but not widowers an annual property tax exemption. The Court said that the intent to ameliorate the effects of past discrimination against women (their disadvantage in the job market) was an important governmental interest to which the law was substantially related. This case came down one year after *Frontiero*. The majority opinion was written by Mr. Justice Douglas, one of the four who argued in *Frontiero* that sex should be a suspect classification. In *Kahn* he explained that the Court had never held gender a suspect classification, and thus the more stringent strict judicial scrutiny standard could not be applied here. The dissent insisted that gender should be a suspect classification and the strict standard would invalidate the Florida law. *Kahn* was the first case to establish the principle that a legitimate attempt to compensate for past discrimination against women—benign discrimination—is sufficient justification for gender-based classifications.

2. *Schlesinger v. Ballard*, 419 U.S. 498 (1975). The Court held that it was not a denial of equal protection to hold a male naval officer to a strict "up or out" system (for lieutenants and below, out when twice passed over for promotion), while guaranteeing a female officer thirteen years before mandatory retirement for lack of promotion. Lieutenant Ballard, a male officer, brought suit contending that the "up or out" regulation violated the due process clause of the Fifth Amendment. But the Court reasoned that since women do not have the same opportunity for professional service as men (they cannot serve in combat positions), the longer tenure granted them was reasonable for

the purpose of providing "fair and equitable career advancement programs."[10] Some commentators considered *Kahn* and *Ballard* to offer women the best of all possible worlds—a Supreme Court ready to strike down statutes and regulations that discriminate against women, yet eager to preserve laws that favor them—while others looked upon them as further protectionism disguising the age-old attitudes about the inferiority of women.[11]

3. *Califano v. Webster,* 430 U.S. 313 (1977). The Court upheld a social security provision in which the elapsed years upon which old age benefits were determined were different for men than for women, giving women a slight advantage. The legislative history of this provision[12] indicated that Congress formulated the scheme in direct response to past discriminatory conditions encountered by working women—specifically, depressed wages and early retirement forced upon them. The Court held that a statute deliberately enacted to redress society's longstanding disparate treatment of women meets the "important governmental objective" test. The statute in this case, according to the Court, was far different from the one in *Goldfarb,* p. 92 *supra,* because it was purposeful affirmative action and not merely the accidental by-product of a traditional way of thinking about females.

4. *Vorchheimer v. School District,* 400 F.Supp. 326 (E.D. Pa. 1975), *rev'd,* 532 F.2d 880 (3d Cir. 1976), *aff'd by an equally divided Court,* 430 U.S. 703 (1977). The Court was equally divided, 4-4 (Mr. Justice Rehnquist was in the hospital with back trouble), and so the judgment of the Court of Appeals of the Third Circuit was affirmed without a Supreme Court opinion. The Court of Appeals upheld a Philadelphia Public School Board policy of operating sex-segregated high schools for academically gifted girls and boys. The School District maintained two "academic" (exclusively college prep and highly selective admissions) high schools: all-male Central High and all-female Philadelphia High School for Girls. Susan Vorchheimer wanted to attend Central High but was denied because she was a girl. The Circuit Court held that since there was no difference in the quality of education at the two schools, there was no discrimination against girls. Because the Supreme Court was equally divided in this case, the issue of sex-segregated schools under the Fourteenth Amendment is still undecided.

5. *Fiallo v. Bell,* 430 U.S. 787 (1977). The Court upheld a provision in the federal Immigration and Nationality Act which gave special immigration preference to parents or children of U.S. citizens or legal permanent residents. The preference extended to the natural mother but not the natural father of illegitimate children who are citizens or legal permanent residents. The holding in *Fiallo v. Bell* was influenced by the broad discretion that the federal government enjoys in dealing with matters of immigration and citizenship.[13] If this case had not involved the exercise by Congress of its powers over immigration, it probably would have been decided the other way.

6. *Parham v. Hughes,* 441 U.S. 347 (1979). The Court upheld a Georgia statute which permits a mother of an illegitimate child, or the father if he has legitimated the child and there is no mother, to sue for the wrongful death of the child, but not a father who has not legitimated the child. Four of the justices said that the statute distinguishes, not between males and females, but between fathers who have legitimated their children and those who have not. Mr. Justice Powell, in a concurring opinion, said that the statute constitutes

sex discrimination, but it is permissible because it is substantially related to the important governmental objective of avoiding problems of proving paternity. It is interesting to compare this case with *Caban v. Mohammed,* p. 92 *supra,* which was decided on the same day as this case. In *Caban* Mr. Justice Powell cast the deciding vote to invalidate a law permitting unwed mothers but not unwed fathers to block the adoption of their children. The discrimination in *Caban* was not permissible, he said, because the problems of proving paternity could be overcome in other ways.

7. *Personnel Administrator of Massachusetts v. Feeney,* 442 U.S. 256 (1979). The Court upheld a Massachusetts veterans preference statute in spite of the fact that it operated overwhelmingly in favor of males. The law decreed that disabled veterans, veterans, and surviving spouses and surviving parents of veterans be ranked above all other candidates for official civil service jobs. Helen Feeney applied for at least two jobs in which veterans with lower qualification scores were appointed over her merely because they were veterans. She claimed, with convincing proof, that because of the discrimination against the enlistment of women in the armed forces, the statute operates overwhelmingly in favor of males. The Court ruled, however, that in order for a sex-neutral statute with disproportionately adverse effects on women to be declared unconstitutional, the Court must find not only a discriminatory effect but also a discriminatory purpose behind the statute. That is, it must find that the legislature drafted the statute because of, not merely in spite of, its adverse effects on the group. In this holding, the Court followed the same standard used in racial discrimination cases.[14]

C. Cases Dealing with Pregnancy

In addition to the cases involving sex-discrimination, a number have also been heard involving the discriminatory treatment of pregnant women. The pregnancy question, however, has not been treated by the Court as an equal protection issue. As in sex discrimination cases, the Court has considered each case individually on its merits, upholding some classifications and invalidating others. A brief summary of the decisions in these cases follows.

Working Pregnant Women. Pregnant women are capable of working until their physician decides otherwise. In *Board of Education v. La Fleur,* 414 U.S. 632 (1974), the Court held that school teachers may not be dismissed or placed on forced leave arbitrarily at a fixed stage of pregnancy well in advance of the expected delivery date. To do so would create an irrebuttable presumption in conflict with due process.[15] The individual woman is therefore entitled to a hearing to determine whether pregnancy adversely affects her ability to perform her job. On that same basis the Court also decided in *Turner v. Department of Employment Security,* 423 U.S. 44 (1975), that pregnant women who are ready, willing, and able to work may not be denied unemployment compensation when jobs are closed to them.

Disability Benefits. The Court held in *General Electric Co. v. Gilbert,* 429 U.S. 125 (1976), and *Geduldig v. Aiello,* 417 U.S. 484 (1974), that the exclusion of pregnancy from a disability benefits program is not gender-based discrimination at all but is merely the exclusion of a class of disability from coverage. After all, nonpregnant *persons* are treated alike. But *National Gas Co.*

v. Satty, 434 U.S. 136 (1977), said that there is a difference between excluding pregnancy from benefit programs and placing burdens on pregnant women. It held unlawful under Title VII of the Civil Rights Act of 1964[16] an employer's practice of depriving women on pregnancy leave of their accumulated seniority.

Thus, the current state of the law appears to be that employers cannot force a woman to take leave at some arbitrary stage of pregnancy, and they cannot place additional burdens upon women because of pregnancy; but they can deny disability benefits on account of pregnancy.

D. Abortion

Many commentators and women's rights activists consider abortion a part of the sex equality issue.[17] In landmark rulings in 1973, *Roe v. Wade,* 410 U.S. 113 (1973), and *Doe v. Bolton,* 410 U.S. 179 (1973), the Court held that some antiabortion laws are unwarranted state intrusions into the decision of a woman and her doctor to terminate a pregnancy. But the opinions barely mention women's rights; they are not tied to any equal protection or equal rights theory. Rather, the Court derived a concept of privacy and personal autonomy from the due process guarantee. In *Planned Parenthood v. Danforth,* 428 U.S. 52 (1976), the Court went even further and invalidated requirements that consent to an abortion be obtained from either the husband or the parents of the pregnant woman.

In three decisions in 1977, *Beal v. Doe,* 432 U.S. 438 (1977); *Maher v. Roe,* 432 U.S. 464 (1977); *Poelker v. Doe,* 432 U.S. 519 (1977), the Court declared that although the government cannot interfere with a woman's decision to have an abortion, the state is not required to pay for it. This qualification was reinforced recently in *Williams v. Zbaraz,* 48 USLW 4957 (Sup. Ct. 1980) and *Harris v. McRae,* 48 USLW 4941 (Sup. Ct. 1980), in which the Court again held that neither the state nor the federal government is required to fund all abortions for the indigent even though it funds some, as in the case of rape, incest, or endangered health of the mother.

E. Title VII Cases

Title VII of the Civil Rights Act of 1964[18] states that it is unlawful "to discriminate against any individual with respect to compensation, terms, conditions, or privileges of employment, because of such individual's race, color, sex, or national origin." The question of sex discrimination in employment has been much litigated since the passage of this law and a few of the cases have reached the Supreme Court. Although these cases have not been decided on constitutional grounds, they are instructive of the Court's attitude regarding sex discrimination under current law.

The cases of *General Electric Co. v. Gilbert* and *National Gas Co. v. Satty,* discussed above, both dealing with the pregnancy issue, were decided under Title VII.

In *Fitzpatrick v. Bitzer,* 427 U.S. 445 (1976), male employees of the state of Connecticut brought a class action suit alleging that the state's retirement benefit plan discriminated against them because of their sex, in violation of

Title VII. Although the lower court ruled in favor of the employees, it refused to grant their request for retroactive retirement benefits and attorney's fees. Such an award, the lower court reasoned, would constitute a recovery of money from the state's treasury and thus violate the Eleventh Amendment and the principle of sovereign immunity. The Supreme Court, however, ruled that the Eleventh Amendment and its principle of state sovereignty are limited by the enforcement provisions of the Fourteenth Amendment. Because of that provision, Congress may provide for suits against states under Title VII that would be constitutionally impermissible in other contexts.

In *Dothard v. Rawlinson,* 433 U.S. 321 (1977), the Court considered height and weight standards and an outright gender-based classification. An Alabama statute set 120 pounds as the minimum weight and 5'2" as the minimum height for the position of prison guard. In addition, a prison regulation prohibited women from "contact positions" (requiring close proximity to inmates). The Court invalidated the height and weight standards because the state did not show a relationship between the requirements and good job performance. Interestingly, though, the Court upheld the gender-based classification for "contact positions" because of (1) the frequent violence in these prisons, (2) inmate access to guards, (3) understaffing, and (4) the substantial number of sex offenders mixed in with the other prisoners. It is apparent that this decision is narrowly limited to the fact situation in the case.

City of Los Angeles Dept. of Water and Power v. Manhart, 435 U.S. 702 (1978), involved a pension fund and actuarial statistics. The Los Angeles Department of Water and Power required female employees to make larger contributions than males to its pension fund because mortality tables and experience showed that women live longer than men and thus, as a class, receive pension payments longer than males. The Court, in its decision invalidating that requirement, held that the language of Title VII, making it unlawful to "discriminate against any *individual*" because of sex, precludes treating individuals as simply components of a class.

B

Appendix
State Equal Rights Provisions
and Language of State Court Opinions
Concerning Governing Standard

Alaska

Constitutional Provision

Article I, §3
No person is to be denied the enjoyment of any civil or political right because of race, color, creed, sex, or national origin. The legislature shall implement this section.

Cases Indicating the Standard of Judicial Review

Plas v. State, 598 P.2d 966, 968 (Alaska 1979)
It is apparent that the [prostitution] statute invidiously discriminates against females. The offense of prostitution is capable of being committed by a male, but is nowhere made criminal by the statute. In striking at prostitution the legislation singles out only the female body as the critical physical element of the crime. In view of gender neutrality required by article I, section 3, of the Alaska Constitution, the means used to accomplish the legislative end lacks rational justification. In creating criminal offenses it is particularly important that any distinctions as to gender rest upon some logical justification having a basis in the actual conditions of human life. In our view the statute is unconstitutional insofar as it limits its operation to selling of only a female body.

Colorado

Constitutional Provision

Article II, §29
Equality of the sexes. Equality of rights under the law shall not be denied or abridged by the state of Colorado or any of its political subdivisions on account of sex.

Cases Indicating the Standard of Judicial Review

People v. Salinas, 191 Colo. 171, 551 P.2d 703, 706 (1976)
This [equal rights] amendment prohibits unequal treatment based exclusively on the circumstance of sex, social stereotypes connected with gender, and culturally induced dissimilarities. However, it does not prohibit differential treatment among the sexes when, as here, that treatment is reasonably and genuinely based on physical characteristics unique to just one sex.

People v. Barger, 191 Colo. 152, 550 P.2d 1281, 1283 (1976)
We likewise reject the contention that the statute in question violates the Equal Rights Amendment. Colo. Const., Art. II, Sec. 29. While we agree with defendant that legislative classifications predicated on sexual status must receive the closest judicial scrutiny, we conclude that section 40-3-402(1)(a) passes constitutional muster under that test.

Connecticut

Constitutional Provision

Article I, §20
No person shall be denied the equal protection of the law nor be subjected to segregation or discrimination in the exercise or enjoyment of his civil or political rights because of religion, race, color, ancestry, national origin or sex.

Cases Indicating the Standard of Judicial Review

Lockwood v. Killian, 172 Conn. 496, 375 A.2d 998, 1001 (1977)
For the purposes of this case, the constitution of Connecticut, article first, §20, is the state counterpart of the equal protection clause of the fourteenth amendment to the constitution of the United States. These provisions of the federal and state constitutions "have the same meaning and impose similar constitutional limitations."

Hawaii

Constitutional Provision

Article I, §4
No person shall be deprived of life, liberty or property without due process of law, nor be denied the equal protection of the laws, nor be denied the enjoyment of his civil rights or be discriminated against in the exercise thereof because of race, religion, sex or ancestry.

Article I, §21
Equality of rights under the law shall not be denied or abridged by the State on account of sex.

Cases Indicating the Standard of Judicial Review

Holdman v. Olim, 59 Hawaii 346, 581 P.2d 1164, 1168–69 (1978)

We need not deal finally with that issue, and reserve it for future consideration, since we conclude that the compelling state interest test would be satisfied in this case if it were held to be applicable. It is apparent that the bar against sex-based classification is not absolute under the strictest test which has been applied under the Fourteenth Amendment. Even if a sex-based classification is deemed to be suspect and thus subject to stricter scrutiny under the equal protection clause of Article I, Section 4, than under the equal protection clause of the Fourteenth Amendment, such scrutiny involves consideration of whether the use of the suspect classification is necessary to protect a compelling state interest. We do not use these terms to define the limits to be drawn under the test of strict scrutiny, but only to indicate that state action which is challenged under the equal protection clause will survive strict scrutiny if the state demonstrates a sufficiently important interest and employs means which are closely enough drawn.

... We have concluded that the treatment of which appellant complains withstands the test of strict scrutiny by reason of a compelling state interest. We are not prepared to hold in this case that, if a more stringent test should be applied under Article I, Section 21, the prohibition of that section is so absolute that it is not subject to the exception for physical characteristics unique to only one sex.

Illinois

Constitutional Provision

Article I, §18

The equal protection of the laws shall not be denied or abridged on account of sex by the State or its units of local government and school districts.

Cases Indicating the Standard of Judicial Review

People v. Boyer, 24 Ill. App.3d 671, 321 N.E.2d 312, 314 (1974)

Inclusion of article I, section 18 [the equal rights amendment] required the court to hold that a classification based upon sex is a "suspect classification" and must be able to withstand "strict judicial scrutiny" to be held valid.

Maryland

Constitutional Provision

Declaration of Rights, Art. 46

Equality of rights under the law shall not be abridged or denied because of sex.

Cases Indicating the Standard of Judicial Review

Rand v. Rand, 280 Md. 508, 374 A.2d 900, 902–3 (1977)
The words of the E.R.A. are clear and unambiguous; they say without equivocation that "Equality of rights under the law shall not be abridged or denied because of sex." This language mandating equality of rights can only mean that sex is not a factor.

Coleman v. Maryland, 37 Md. App. 322, 377 A.2d 553, 556 (1977)
In *Rand v. Rand,* Chief Judge Murphy pointed out that [gender-based] distinctions are now absolutely forbidden.

See also Kline v. Ansell, No. 96, Slip Op. (Ct. of App. Md. May 26, 1980).

Massachusetts

Constitutional Provision

Part 1, Article 6
Equality under the law shall not be denied or abridged because of sex, race, color, creed or national origin.

Cases Indicating the Standard of Judicial Review

Commonwealth v. King, 1977 Mass. Adv. Sh. 2636, 372 N.E.2d 196, 206 (1977)
Article 106 incorporates into our State Constitution an express prohibition of discrimination on the basis of sex, grouping it with other prohibited bases for discrimination which are subject to strict judicial scrutiny. All the categorical bases listed therein logically are subject to the same degree of judicial scrutiny, and in our opinion that degree of scrutiny must be at least as strict as the scrutiny required by the Fourteenth Amendment for racial classifications. Therefore, we conclude that the people of Massachusetts view sex discrimination with the same vigorous disapproval as they view racial, ethnic, and religious discrimination.

Attorney General v. Massachusetts Interscholastic Athletic Ass'n., Inc., 1979 Mass. Adv. Sh. 1584, 393 N.E.2d 284, 291 (1979)
We have held under ERA that classifications on the basis of sex are subject to a degree of constitutional scrutiny "at least as strict as the scrutiny required by the Fourteenth Amendment for racial classifications."

Montana

Constitutional Provision

Article II, §4
The dignity of the human being is inviolable. No person shall be denied the equal protection of the laws. Neither the state nor any person, firm, corporation, or institution shall discriminate against any person in the exercise of his civil or political rights on account of race, color, sex, culture, social origin or condition, or political or religious ideas.

Cases Indicating the Standard of Judicial Review

State v. Craig, 169 Mont. 150, 545 P.2d 649, 652-53 (1976)
Defendant contends the pre-1975 version of the statute is an unconstitutionally arbitrary distinction based solely upon sex. It is argued the ... section violates the equal protection clause of the Fourteenth Amendment to the United States Constitution and the equal protection provision of Article II, Section 4, 1972 Montana Constitution.

The United States Supreme Court ... has set down the following rules to test whether a classification is arbitrary and consequently denies equal protection of the laws:
1. The equal-protection clause of the 14th Amendment does not take from the state the power to classify in the adoption of police laws, but admits of the exercise of a wide scope of discretion in that regard, and avoids what is done only when it is without any reasonable basis, and therefore is purely arbitrary. 2. A classification having some reasonable basis does not offend against that clause merely because it is not made with mathematical nicety, or because in practice it results in some inequality. 3. When the classification in such a law is called in question, if any state of facts reasonably can be conceived that would sustain it, the existence of that state of facts at the time the law was enacted must be assumed. 4. One who assails the classification in such a law must carry the burden of showing that it does not rest upon any reasonable basis, but it is essentially arbitrary.

New Hampshire

Constitutional Provision

Part 1, Article 6
Equality of rights under the law shall not be denied or abridged by this state on account of race, creed, color, sex or national origin.

Cases Indicating the Standard of Judicial Review

Buckner v. Buckner, 415 A.2d 871, 872 (1980)
Moreover, *Hartnett* was decided at a time when the doctrine of equal protection based on gender had not advanced to the stage it oc-

cupies today. The United States Supreme Court has determined that it is a denial of equal protection for a statute to authorize alimony for a wife but not for a husband. *Orr v. Orr,* 440 U.S. 268 (1979). If the statutes of this State should be construed to treat husbands less favorably than wives, they would be invalid under the Constitution of the United States. Furthermore, N.H. Const. Pt. 1, Art. 11 would prohibit discrimination on account of sex.

New Mexico

Constitutional Provision

Article 2, §18
No person shall be deprived of life, liberty or property without due process of law; nor shall any person be denied equal protection of the laws. Equality of rights under law shall not be denied on account of the sex of any person.

Cases Indicating the Standard of Judicial Review

No case law establishing a standard of judicial review.

Pennsylvania

Constitutional Provision

Article I, §28
Equality of rights under the law shall not be denied or abridged in the Commonwealth of Pennsylvania because of the sex of the individual.

Cases Indicating the Standard of Judicial Review

Henderson v. Henderson, 458 Pa. 97, 327 A.2d 60, 62 (1974)
The thrust of the Equal Rights Amendment is to insure equality of rights under the law and to eliminate sex as a basis for distinction. The sex of citizens of this Commonwealth is no longer a permissible factor in the determination of their legal rights and legal responsibilities. The law will not impose different benefits or different burdens upon the members of a society based on the fact that they may be man or woman.

DeFlorido v. DeFlorido, 459 Pa. 641, 331 A.2d 174, 179 (1975)
With the passage of the Equal Rights Amendment, this Court has striven to insure the equality of rights under the law and to eliminate sex as a basis for distinction.

Commonwealth v. Pennsylvania Interscholastic Athletic Ass'n, 18 Pa.Commw.Ct.45, 334 A.2d 839, 843 (1975)

From the dissenting opinion:

I dissent. In striking down the PIAA regulation here in issue on plaintiff's motion for summary judgment and without evidentiary hearing as violative of Article I, Section 28, of our Constitution, it is inescapable in my view that the majority has extruded prior decisions of our Supreme Court to the absonant conclusion that under no circumstances and under no conditions—with the possible exception of our interpersonal relationships—can there be a rational basis for distinction or classification as between the sexes.

Texas

Constitutional Provision

Article I, §3(a)

Equality under the law shall not be denied or abridged because of sex, race, color, creed, or national origin.

Cases Indicating the Standard of Judicial Review

Mercer v. Board of Trustees, 538 S.W.2d 201, 206 (Tex. Civ. App. 1976)

Any classification based upon sex is a suspect classification, and any law or regulation that classifies persons for different treatment on the basis of their sex is subject to strictest judicial scrutiny. Any such classification must fall unless the party defending it can show that it is required by (1) physical characteristics, (2) other constitutionally protected rights such as the right of privacy, or (3) other "compelling reasons."

Utah

Constitutional Provision

Article IV, §1*

The rights of citizens of the State of Utah to vote and hold office shall not be denied or abridged on account of sex. Both male and female citizens of this State shall enjoy equally all civil, political and religious rights and privileges.

Cases Indicating the Standard of Judicial Review

In re Baer, 562 P.2d 614, 615, *appeal dismissed,* 434 U.S. 805 (1977)

The constitutional issue presented by respondents requires a determination whether the allowance of a distributive share only for widows is a discriminatory classification. Such a classification may be upheld if it bears a fair and substantial relation to a legitimate state purpose.

---

*Utah included this provision in its original constitution, and this is not technically an equal rights *amendment.*

Virginia

Constitutional Provision

Article I, §11
[T]he right to be free from any governmental discrimination upon the basis of religious conviction, race, color, sex, or national origin shall not be abridged, except that the mere separation of the sexes shall not be considered discrimination.

Cases Indicating the Standard of Judicial Review

Archer v. Mayes, 213 Va. 633, 194 S.E.2d 707, 711 (1973)
Appellants also say that the statutory exemption runs afoul of Article I, Section 11, of the 1971 Constitution of Virginia prohibiting "any governmental discrimination upon the basis of . . . sex." This provision prohibits invidious, arbitrary discrimination upon the basis of sex. It is no broader than the equal protection clause of the Fourteenth Amendment to the Constitution of the United States. Where a statute is based on a reasonable classification that bears a rational relationship to the objective of the State, as here, there is no impermissible discrimination under the Constitution of Virginia.

Washington

Constitutional Provision

Article 31, §1
Equality of rights and responsibility under the law shall not be denied or abridged on account of sex.

Cases Indicating the Standard of Judicial Review

Darrin v. Gould, 85 Wash.2d 859, 540 P.2d 882, 889, 893 (1975)
Whatever doubts on that score might have been formerly entertained, Const. art. 31 [the equal rights amendment] added something to the prior prevailing law by eliminating otherwise permissible sex discrimination if the rational relationship or strict scrutiny tests were met.
. . . [U]nder our ERA discrimination on account of sex is forbidden.

Marchioro v. Chaney, 90 Wash.2d 298, 582 P.2d 487, 491, (1978), *aff'd,* 442 U.S. 191 (1979)
Under the equal rights amendment, the equal protection/suspect classification test is replaced by the single criterion: Is the classification by sex discriminatory? or, in the language of the amendment, Has equality been denied or abridged on account of sex? (In the language of *Darrin v. Gould,* "under our ERA discrimination on account of sex is forbidden.")

The thrust of the equal rights amendment is to end special treatment for or discrimination against either sex.

Wyoming

Constitutional Provision

Article I, §3*
Since equality in the enjoyment of natural and civil rights is only made sure through political equality, the laws of this state affecting the political rights and privileges of its citizens shall be without distinction of race, color, sex, or any circumstance or condition whatsoever other than individual incompetency, or unworthiness duly ascertained by a court of competent jurisdiction.

Cases Indicating the Standard of Judicial Review

No case law establishing a standard of judicial review.

---

*Wyoming included this provision in its original constitution, and this is not technically an equal rights *amendment*.

Notes

Citations are generally in the style set forth in *A Uniform System of Citation*, 12th ed. (Cambridge: Harvard Law Review Association, 1976). Mention of one convention here is appropriate, particularly for researchers unfamiliar with legal style. When citations refer to text material *in this volume*, or to other sources cited *in these notes*, *supra* is used to indicate material or notes previously cited, and *infra* is used to indicate material or notes cited later.

Chapter 1

1. For an excellent general discussion of the legal status of women throughout this nation's history, see L. Kanowitz, *Women and the Law* (1969).

2. Only in two special situations were women impaneled on the jury: (1) when a widow claimed to be pregnant and a question of inheritance arose; and (2) when a woman under sentence of death pleaded for a stay of execution until her child was born. *Note, Court—Women Jurors—Automatic Exemption*, 36 Tul. L.Rev. 858 (1962), citing 3 Blackstone, *Commentaries* *363, and 4 Blackstone, *Commentaries* *394.

3. Blackstone, *Commentaries* *442.

4. *The Lawes Resolution of Womens Rights* (London 1632), quoted in E. Flexner, *Century of Struggle* 7–8 (1973).

5. "In Massachusetts Judge Buller defined the legal instrument as a 'stick no thicker than my thumb,' and in New York the courts upheld a worthy Methodist exhorter who beat his wife with a horsewhip every few weeks in order to keep her in proper subjection and prevent her scolding." A. Tyler, *Freedom's Ferment* 426 (1944).

6. Blackstone, *Commentaries* *445.

7. 2 J. Winthrop, *Winthrop's Journal: "History of New England", 1630–1649*, at 225 (1953).

8. *Root of Bitterness: Documents of the Social History of American Women* 34 (N. Cott ed. 1972).

9. K. Lockridge, *Literacy in Colonial New England*, pp. 38–42, 57–58 (1974) as cited in N. F. Cott, *The Bonds of Womanhood* 102–3 (1977).

10. A. G. Spencer, *Woman's Share in Social Culture* (1912) reprinted in M. Schneir, *Feminism: The Essential Historical Writings* 274–75 (1972) [hereinafter cited as Schneir, *Feminism*].

11. Thomas Jefferson, quoted in M. Gruberg, *Women in American Politics* 4 (1968).

12. Quoted in Schneir, *Feminism, supra* note 10, at 3–4.

13. E. Hahn, *Once upon a Pedestal* 20 (1974).

14. R. Riegal, *American Women* 17 (1970).

15. A. de Tocqueville, 2 *Democracy in America* 252 (Reeve Trans. 1961).

16. Kanowitz, *supra* note 1, at 40.

17. Declaration of Sentiments and Resolutions, Seneca Falls, reprinted in Schneir, *Feminism, supra* note 10, at 77–80.

18. U.S. Const. amend. XIV, §2 (emphasis added).

19. E. Flexner, *Century of Struggle* 144 (1973).

20. Prior to the Fourteenth Amendment, there was a due process guarantee in the Fifth Amendment, but it was binding only on the federal government. The Fourteenth Amendment made the due process guarantee binding on state governments.

Chapter 2

1. *Bolling v. Sharpe,* 347 U.S. 497 (1954). *See also Weinberger v. Wiesenfeld,* 420 U.S. 636, 638 n.2 (1975), where the Court says: "This Court's approach to Fifth Amendment Equal Protection claims has always been precisely the same as to Equal Protection claims under the Fourteenth Amendment."

2. This state action doctrine is discussed in Chapter 14 of R. E. Lee, *With Liberty for All: A Study of the United States Constitution* (Provo, Utah: Brigham Young University Press, forthcoming) [hereinafter cited as Lee].

3. There is some indication in the legislative history of the Equal Rights Amendment, however, to the contrary. See *Equal Rights for Men and Women 1971:* Hearings on H.J.Res. 35, 208, and Related Bills, and H.R. 916 and Related Bills before Subcomm. No. 4 of the Committee on the Judiciary, 92d Cong., 1st Sess. 303–4 (1971) [hereinafter cited as *House Hearings*].

4. *See Railway Express Agency v. New York,* 336 U.S. 106 (1949); *Kotch v. Board of River Pilot Commissioners,* 330 U.S. 552 (1947); *Williamson v. Lee Optical Co.,* 348 U.S. 483 (1955).

5. 274 U.S. 200, 208 (1927).

6. *See* Lee, *supra* note 2, ch. 2, at ch. 14 for a more thorough discussion of the three suspect classifications, and what appear to be developing exceptions to alienage as a suspect classification.

Chapter 3

1. The case was *Reed v. Reed,* 404 U.S. 71 (1971), which is discussed at p. 26 *infra.*

2. The first substantive guarantee of the Fourteenth Amendment is commonly called the "privileges and immunities clause," although the amend-

ment itself refers to privileges *or* immunities. The amendment reads: "No State shall make or enforce any law which shall abridge the privileges or immunities of citizens of the United States." U.S. Const. amend. XIV, §1.

3. 83 U.S. (16 Wall.) 36 (1873).

4. *Id.* at 81.

5. *Id.* at 78–79 (emphasis added).

6. McGovney, *Privileges or Immunities Clause—Fourteenth Amendment,* 4 Iowa L.Bull. 219 (1918).

7. 83 U.S. (16 Wall.) 130 (1873).

8. *Id.* at 132.

9. *Id.* at 133–37.

10. *Id.* at 135.

11. *Id.* at 139. Although *Bradwell* was argued before the Court prior to the *Slaughterhouse* argument, *Slaughterhouse* was decided first and became the precedent for the *Bradwell* decision.

12. *Id.* at 141. C. Corker, in 53 Wash.L.Rev. 215 (1978), concludes that the infamous Bradley concurrence in *Bradwell* has had a far-reaching and unintended side effect. In Professor Corker's view, Justice Bradley's dissent in the *Slaughterhouse Cases*—asserting that the right to pursue a common vocation was included within the privileges and immunities of U.S. citizens—might have emerged later as the prevailing view but for the fact that it was discredited by his *Bradwell* opinion the following day. Whatever the merits of this view, it is paradoxical that *Slaughterhouse,* with its narrowest of possible majorities and a vigorous dissent, remains the law of the land regarding the Fourteenth Amendment's privileges and immunities clause, while *Bradwell,* an eight-to-one decision with no written dissent, is today no more than an historic artifact, universally discredited.

13. 88 U.S. (21 Wall.) 162 (1874).

14. *Id.* at 164.

15. 154 U.S. 166 (1894).

16. *Id.* at 117.

17. 192 U.S. 108 (1904).

18. Brief for Plaintiff at 16–17, 192 U.S. 108 (1904).

19. *Id.* at 27, 30, 32, 33.

20. *Id.* at 27.

21. *Id.* at 30.

22. For a general discussion of the requirement that the plaintiff have standing to sue, *see* Lee, *supra* note 2, ch. 2, at ch. 18.

23. 192 U.S. at 112.

24. *Id.* at 114.

25. 137 U.S. 86 (1890).

26. 192 U.S. at 115; 137 U.S. at 91.

27. The due process clause of the Fourteenth Amendment reads: "[N]or shall any state deprive any person of life, liberty, or property without due process of law." U.S. Const. amend. XIV §1.

28. 208 U.S. 412 (1908).

29. *See* Lee, *supra* note 2, ch. 2, at chs. 15 & 17.

30. 1903 Or. Laws.

31. 198 U.S. 45 (1905).

32. *See* Lee, *supra* note 2, ch. 2, at chs. 15 & 17.

33. 208 U.S. at 421.

34. 261 U.S. 525 (1923).

35. *Id.* at 553.

36. The opinion observes: "In the second case the appellee, a woman twenty-one years of age, was employed by the Congress Hall Hotel Company as an elevator operator, at a salary of thirty-five dollars per month and two meals a day. She alleges that the work was light and healthful, the hours short, with surroundings clean and moral, and that she was anxious to continue it for the compensation she was receiving and that she did not earn more. Her services were satisfactory to the hotel company and it would have been glad to retain her but was obliged to dispense with her services by reason of the order of the board and on account of the penalties prescribed by the act. The wages received by this appellee were the best she was able to obtain for any work she was capable of performing and the enforcement of the order, she alleges, deprived her of such employment and wages. She further averred that she could not secure any other position at which she could make a living, with as good physical and moral surroundings, and earn as good wages, and that she was desirous of continuing and would continue the employment but for the order of the board." (*Id.* at 542–43.)

37. 300 U.S. 379 (1937). About eight months after the decision in *West Coast Hotel Co. v. Parrish,* the Supreme Court, in *Breedlove v. Suttles,* 302 US 277 (1937), rejected an attack on the Georgia poll tax. One of the bases for the constitutional challenge in *Breedlove* was that women were exempted from the poll tax unless they registered for voting. The Court reasoned: "In view of burdens necessarily borne by [women] for the preservation of the race, the state reasonably may exempt them from poll taxes." 302 U.S. at 282.

Chapter 4

1. 335 U.S. 464 (1948).

2. *Nadroski v. Same,* 74 F.Supp. 735 (E.D. Mich. 1947).

3. 335 U.S. at 465.

4. *Id.*

5. *Id.* at 465–66.

6. *Id.* at 468.

7. *Id.* at 466 (emphasis added).

8. *Goesaert v. Cleary,* 74 F.Supp. 735 (E.D. Mich. 1947) (emphasis added).

9. 368 U.S. 57 (1961).

10. *Id.* at 61–62.

11. Fla. Stat. §40.04(1) (1959).

12. 419 U.S. 522 (1975).

13. *Id.* at 537.

14. 404 U.S. 71 (1971).

15. Jurisdiction was noted on March 1, 1971. 401 U.S. 934 (1971). The ERA hearings were held March 24, 25, and 31, and April 1, 2, and 5, 1971. S.Rep. No. 689, 92d Cong., 2d Sess. 5 (1972) [hereinafter cited as *Senate Report*]. The *Reed v. Reed* opinion was handed down November 22, 1971.

16. *House Hearings, supra* note 3, ch. 2, at 36–38, 344–45, 400.

17. Idaho Code, §15-314 (1948).

18. 404 U.S. at 76.

19. *Id.* at 75 (emphasis added).

20. 411 U.S. 677 (1973).

21. Because the case involved a federal rather than a state statute, and because the Fourteenth Amendment on its face applies only to states, the Court relied on the Fifth Amendment, which is binding on the federal government and whose due process clause has been held to "incorporate" the equality standards of the Fourteenth Amendment.

22. 411 U.S. at 682.

23. *Id.*

24. *Id.* at 692. Justice Stewart's brief opinion stated that he "concurs in the judgment, agreeing that the statutes before us work an invidious discrimination in violation of the Constitution." *Id.* at 691. Justice Rehnquist dissented. *Id.*

25. 429 U.S. 190 (1976).

26. *Id.* at 197 (emphasis added).

27. *Id.* at n. 8.

28. *Id.*

29. "It is no requirement of equal protection that all evils of the same genus be eradicated or none at all." *Railway Express Agency v. New York,* 336 U.S. 106, 110 (1949), citing *Central Lumber Co. v. South Dakota,* 226 U.S. 157, 160 (1912).

30. *See* Lee, *supra* note 2, ch. 2, at ch. 14.

31. Probably the most extreme example of deference to the legislature in finding an acceptable relationship between the means and the end was in *Railway Express Agency v. New York,* 336 U.S. 106 (1949), discussed in Lee, *supra* note 2, ch. 2, at ch. 14.

32. 443 U.S. 76 (1979).

33. 441 U.S. 380 (1979).

34. 440 U.S. 268 (1979).

35. 420 U.S. 636 (1975).

36. *University of California Regents v. Bakke,* 438 U.S. 265 (1978); *Steel Workers v. Weber,* 442 U.S. 927 (1979).

37. *Califano v. Webster,* 430 U.S. 313 (1977); *Schlesinger v. Ballard,* 419 U.S. 498 (1975); *Kahn v. Shevin,* 416 U.S. 351 (1974).

38. *Califano v. Goldfarb,* 430 U.S. 199 (1977) ("archaic and overbroad" generalizations); *Stanton v. Stanton,* 421 U.S. 7 (1975).

Chapter 5

1. 88 U.S. (21 Wall.) 162 (1874). The other two were the Eleventh Amendment, *Worcester v. Georgia,* 31 U.S. (6 Pet.) 515 (1836), and the Sixteenth Amendment, *Pollock v. Farmer's Loan and Trust Co.,* 157 U.S. 429 (1895), *aff'd on rehearing,* 158 U.S. 601 (1895).

2. W. Chafe, *The American Woman* 112–13 (1972). "No issue divided women's organizations more than the Equal Rights Amendment to the Constitution.... Endorsed by one wing of the suffrage movement and opposed by the other, it immediately became a focal point of controversy. Mary Anderson of the Women's Bureau denounced it as 'vicious,' 'doctrinaire,' and 'a kind of hysterical feminism with a slogan for a program.' Other suffragists viewed it as a direct threat to all the special legislation passed to protect women. For decades the amendment embroiled the women's movement in bitter strife and as much as anything else prevented the development of a united feminist appeal."

3. *Id.* at 113. "The Women's Party (formerly the Congressional Union) constituted the militant wing of the suffrage movement. Its adherents adopted radical tactics, chaining themselves to fences, picketing the White House, and engaging in hunger strikes in prison. NAWSA, on the other hand, sought to cooperate with the government and to work from within to achieve its goals."

4. *Id.* at 119. "By mid-decade [1920s] the two opposing camps were engaged in a bitter war. One side fought for the exclusive goal of female equality; the other side for social reform. One side believed that suffrage was only the first step in the campaign for freedom; the other that the Nineteenth Amendment had substantially finished the task of making women equal to men."

5. Curtis: S.J. Res. 21, 68th Cong., 1st Sess., 65 Cong. Rec. 150 (1923).

    Anthony: H.R.J. Res. 75, 68th Cong., 1st Sess., 65 Cong. Rec. 285 (1923).

6. S.J. Res. 21, *supra* note 5.

7. B. Babcock, A. Freedman, E. Norton, and S. Ross, *Sex Discrimination and the Law* 129 (1975) [hereinafter cited as *Babcock et al*].

8. Congressional hearings on the amendment were held in 1924, 1925 (in both the House and Senate), 1929, 1931, 1932, 1933, 1938, 1945, 1956, 1970, and 1971.

9. *Babcock et al., supra* note 7, at 130. "In the early 1940s, the Senate Committee on the Judiciary began to report the amendment for favorable action on the floor. America's experience in World War II provided strong evidence in the case for the amendment. That war had taken women out of the home in far greater numbers than ever before, and women had shown that they could perform successfully many jobs formerly considered appropriate only for men. There was a sense that by their service to the country women had proved themselves deserving of equal pay for equal work and other legal rights."

10. S.Rep.No. 267, 78th Cong., 1st Sess. (1943).

11. 1943: *Id.*
   1946: S.Rep. No. 1013, 79th Cong., 2nd Sess.
   1948: S.Rep. No. 1208, 80th Cong., 2nd Sess.
   1949: S.Rep. No. 137, 81st Cong., 1st Sess.
   1951: S.Rep. No. 356, 82nd Cong., 1st Sess.
   1953: S.Rep. No. 221, 83rd Cong., 1st Sess.
   1956: S.Rep. No. 1991, 84th Cong., 2nd Sess.
   1957: S.Rep. No. 1150, 85th Cong., 1st Sess.
   1959: S.Rep. No. 303, 86th Cong., 1st Sess.
   1962: S.Rep. No. 2192, 87th Cong., 2nd Sess.
   1964: S.Rep. No. 1558, 88th Cong., 2nd Sess.

12. 92 Cong. Rec. 9223 (1946). The proposed amendment used this same language until 1970. *See also* note 33 *infra*.

13. 96 Cong. Rec. 872 (1950).

14. 99 Cong. Rec. 8974 (1953).

15. 96 Cong. Rec. 738 (1950).

16. Chafe, *supra* note 2, at 188. "The Hayden rider in effect voided the operative intent of the feminist bill and rendered it meaningless. 'My amendment is a revolving door,' Hayden boasted. 'We come in one side and go out the other.' One Washington reporter observed that Hayden 'could put a rider on the Ten Commandments and nullify them completely.' Although the Equal Rights Amendment was passed by the Senate one more time in 1953, with the Hayden rider, the Senate's action effectively buried hopes for its adoption until the late 1960's."

17. 109 Cong. Rec. 19342 (1963).

18. *See* ch. 4 *supra*.

19. *Babcock et al., supra* note 7, at 132.
   "By 1970, this development [Application of the Fourteenth Amendment's equal protection clause to sex-based classifications] no longer seemed imminent, and the drive for passage of the Equal Rights Amendment was revived. In March, the Citizens' Advisory Council on the Status of Women issued a cogent memorandum on the ERA prepared by Mary Eastwood, which moved toward a coherent theory of the Equal Rights Amendment. When the Senate hearings were held in 1970, the Harvard Civil Rights–Civil

Liberties Law Review prevailed upon Norman Dorsen, Thomas I. Emerson, Paul A. Freund, and Philip B. Kurland, four of the law professors who testified (on both sides of the issue), to expand their testimony for publication in a symposium on the ERA, to which Dr. Pauli Murray, Susan C. Ross, and Barbara Kirk Cavanaugh also contributed. In addition, Barbara A. Brown, Professor Emerson, Gail Falk, and Ann E. Freedman collaborated on the previously mentioned article in the Yale Law Journal, which offered a definitive explanation of the impact of the amendment in the four areas of the law which had been the most controversial."

20. Griffiths: H.R.J. Res. 264, 91st Cong., 1st Sess., 115 Cong. Rec. 1144 (1969).

McCarthy: S.J. Res. 61, 91st Cong., 1st Sess., 115 Cong. Rec. 4831 (1969).

21. 116 Cong. Rec. 36864–66 (1970).

22. *The "Equal Rights" Amendment: Hearings on S.J. Res. 61 before the Subcomm. on Constitutional Amendments of the Senate Comm. on the Judiciary*, 91st Cong., 2nd Sess. (1970).

23. *Equal Rights 1970: Hearings on S.J. Res. 61 and S.J. Res. 231 before the Senate Comm. on the Judiciary*, 91st Cong., 2nd Sess. (1970) [hereinafter cited as *Senate Hearings*].

24. 116 Cong. Rec. 28036–37 (1970).

25. Proposed: 116 Cong. Rec. 36317 (1970).
Passed: 36/33, 116 Cong. Rec. 36451 (1970).

26. Proposed: 116 Cong. Rec. 36478–79 (1970).
Passed: 50/20, 116 Cong. Rec. 36505 (1970).

27. N.Y. Times, Oct. 15, 1970, at 31, col. 1.

28. 116 Cong. Rec. 36863–64 (1970).

29. 116 Cong. Rec. 36864–66 (1970).
N.Y. Times, Nov. 12, 1970, at 19, col. 3.

30. The other two times were 1950 and 1953 when the proposed Equal Rights Amendment passed the Senate with the Hayden rider, only to be ignored by the House of Representatives. *See* notes 13 & 14 *supra*.

31. Griffiths: H.R.J. Res. 208, 92nd Cong., 1st Sess., 117 Cong. Rec. 526 (1971).
Cook: S.J. Res. 8 and S.J. Res. 9, 92nd Cong., 1st Sess., 117 Cong. Rec. 272 (1971).

32. The only changes during this period related to either the number of years in which the state must ratify or the number of years between ratification and the effective date.

33. The Equal Rights Amendment proposed in 1971 and passed in 1972 reads as follows:

> Section 1. Equality of rights under the law shall not be
> denied or abridged by the United States or by any State on
> account of sex.

Section 2. *The Congress* shall have the power to enforce, by appropriate legislation, the provisions of this article. [Emphasis added.]

Section 3. This amendment shall take effect two years after the date of ratification.

S.Rep. No. 689, 92nd Cong., 2nd Sess. 2, 117 Cong. Rec. 35398 (1971).

34. *House Hearings, supra* note 3, ch. 2, at 78. "Also, S.J. Res. 8 and 9 and H.J. Res. 208 are changed in one important respect from the equal rights amendments which were introduced last year. The amendments introduced this year give Congress total jurisdiction to enforce the amendment. Last year's proposal split the jurisdiction to enforce the article between the States and Congress. To my mind this is an added reason that the States will never ratify this amendment because it grants to Congress only the right to enact laws that reflect in any way differences in the sexes. Obviously, this is a broad area of jurisdiction which the States will not care to relinquish."

35. *Id.*

36. H.R. Rep. No. 359, 92nd Cong., 1st Sess. 6 (1971) [hereinafter cited as *House Report*].

37. *Senate Report, supra* note 15, ch. 4, at 5.

38. 117 Cong. Rec. 35813 (1971).

39. 117 Cong. Rec. 35815 (1971).

40. *Senate Report, supra* note 15, ch. 4, at 5.

41. *Id.* at 5–6.

42. *Id.* at 19.

43. *Id.* at 5–6. For the content and a discussion of Senator Ervin's amendments, *see* p. 45 *infra.*

44. *Id.* at 1.

45. 118 Cong. Rec. 9598 (1972).

46. S. Rep. No. 126, 95th Cong., 1st Sess. 5 (1977).

47. *House Hearings, supra* note 3, ch. 2, at 41.

48. Legislature of Nebraska, 83d Leg., 1st Sess., Legislative Resolution 9.

49. Tennessee S.J. Res. 29, 88th Gen. Assembly (1974).

50. Idaho H.R. Con. Res. 10, 44th Legis. (1977).

51. Kentucky H.J. Res. 20, 1978 Regular Sess. of the Gen. Assembly (1978).

52. South Dakota S.J. Res. 2, 51st Legis. (1979).

53. This assumes that the procedure is the one that was followed in the case of the Equal Rights Amendment and that has been followed for all of the amendments except the Twenty-first. Article V also provides an alternative procedure for both the initial proposal [a convention called by Congress on application of the legislatures of two-thirds of the states] and for ratification [by conventions in three-fourths of the states]. Article V empowers Congress, as part of its proposal, to designate the required mode of ratification.

54. It is possible that the present count might be thirty-two, rather than thirty-one or thirty-five, because the Kentucky rescission has a peculiar wrinkle. The rescission was enacted by both houses of the Kentucky legislature, but while the governor was out of the state the lieutenant governor cast her veto over it. However, an executive veto probably is invalid with respect to ratification—or rescission—as Article V of the Constitution refers only to approvals of the legislature; that is, executive approval is probably not required either for initial ratification or for rescission. The position that executive approval is probably unnecessary is somewhat strengthened by a U.S. Supreme Court holding that Congress's initial proposal of a new constitutional amendment does not need the signature of the President. *See Hollingsworth v. Virginia,* 3 U.S. (3 Dall.) 378 (1798).

55. *Coleman v. Miller,* 307 U.S. 433 (1939).

56. 256 U.S. 368, 375-76 (1921).

57. U.S. Const. amends. XVIII, XX, XXI, and XXII.

58. U.S. Const. amend. XXIII: 106 Cong. Rec. 12571 (1960).
    U.S. Const. amend. XXIV: 108 Cong. Rec. 17655 (1962).
    U.S. Const. amend. XXV: 111 Cong. Rec. 15212-13 (1965).
    U.S. Const. amend. XXVI: 117 Cong. Rec. 7570 (1971).

59. 117 Cong. Rec. 35308 (1971).

60. 124 Cong. Rec. H8664 (daily ed. Aug. 15, 1978); 124 Cong. Rec. S17,318 (daily ed. Oct. 6, 1978).

61. *Idaho v. Oliver,* Civ. Action No. 79-1097 (D. Idaho).

Chapter 6

1. *See* Lee, *supra* note 2, ch. 2, at chs. 17 & 18.

2. *See Darrin v. Gould,* 85 Wash.2d 859, 540 P.2d 882, 889 (1975); *Lindsay v. Collins,* 96 F.Supp. 994, 998 (D.C. Wyo. 1951); *Louisville Country Club, Inc. v. Gray,* 178 F.Supp. 915, 918 (W.D. Ky. 1959), *aff'd,* 285 F.2d 532 (6th Cir. 1960).

3. Hereinafter this will be referred to as "legislative history." The term *legislative history* usually means the proceedings before a legislature or congress concerning a law that has been enacted by that body. The term is not quite as accurate when used in connection with congressional proceedings related to a constitutional amendment. The reason is that the legislative history of a constitutional amendment really includes not only the congressional proceedings but also those in each of the ratifying states. Nevertheless, the term will be used for convenience' sake to refer to the congressional proceedings.

4. The only case before *Reed v. Reed,* 404 U.S. 71 (1971), that had invalidated a sex-based classification on any grounds was *Adkins v. Childrens Hospital,* 261 U.S. 525 (1923), which was overruled fifteen years later. *See* ch. 4 *supra.*

5. *House Hearings, supra* note 3, ch. 2, at 167, 169-72, 344-45, 357, 361, 516, 530-31, and 539.

6. *Id.* at 307, 357, and 584; 117 Cong. Rec. 35299-300 (1971).

7. 411 U.S. 677 (1973).

8. *Id.* at 692 (emphasis added).

9. The three concurring justices and their respective ages as of 1980 are Chief Justice Burger, age 73 (9/17/07); Justice Powell, age 73 (9/19/07); and Justice Blackmun, age 72 (11/12/08). (*International Who's Who* 1979–80 [43d ed. 1980]).

10. *Mercer v. Board of Trustees,* 538 S.W.2d 201 (Tex. Civ. App. 1976).

11. 83 U.S. (16 Wall.) 130 (1873). *See* pp. 16–17 *supra.*

12. The Wiggins amendments are discussed in the following subsection. The first of those added the words "of any person" after the word "rights" in the first section of House Joint Resolution 208. *House Report, supra* note 36, ch. 5, at 1.

13. *House Report, supra* note 36, ch. 5, at 5.

14. *Id.* at 1. The new section would have been section 2, with the existing sections 2 and 3 becoming 3 and 4.

15. *Id.* at 2.

16. *Id.* at 3.

17. *Id.* at 3–4.

18. *Id.* at 3.

19. *Id.* at 6.

20. *Id.* at 5.

21. 117 Cong. Rec. 35813 (1971).

22. *Senate Report, supra* note 15, ch. 4, at 52.

23. *Id.* at 5.

24. *Id.* at 19.

25. *Id.* at 6.

26. *Id.*

27. 116 Cong. Rec. 36834–66 (1970).

28. *Senate Report, supra* note 15, ch. 4, at 20.

29. *Id.* at 35.

30. *Id.*

31. *House Hearings, supra* note 3, ch. 2, at 399–414. *Equal Rights Amendment Extension: Hearings on S.J. Res. 134 before the Subcomm. on the Constitution of the Senate Comm. on the Judiciary,* 95th Cong., 2d Sess. 114–41 (1978) [hereinafter cited as *Extension Hearings*].

32. *House Hearings, supra* note 3, ch. 2, at 401.

33. *Id.*

34. *Id.* at 402 (emphasis added).

35. *Id.* at 406.

36. *Id.* at 402.

37. *Id.*

38. *Id.*

39. *Id.*

40. *Id.*

41. 381 U.S. 479 (1965). *See also, Roe v. Wade,* 410 U.S. 113 (1973); *Planned Parenthood v. Danforth,* 428 U.S. 52 (1976).

42. Brown, Emerson, Falk, & Freedman, *The Equal Rights Amendment: A Constitutional Basis for Equal Rights for Women,* 80 Yale L.J. 871, 894 [hereinafter cited as Brown, Emerson, *et al.*].

43. *Senate Report, supra* note 15, ch. 4, at 35–36.

44. ·*House Report, supra* note 36, ch. 5, at 6.

45. A report entitled *A Commentary on the Effect of the Equal Rights Amendment on State Laws and Institutions,* prepared for the California Commission on the Status of Women's Equal Rights Amendment Project (hereinafter referred to as *Commentary*), expresses the view that "although it cannot be predicted with certainty what standard the Supreme Court will use to interpret the Equal Rights Amendment in the first cases which come before it after the Amendment's passage, it seems likely that the absolute prohibition approach contained in the Yale article will be followed."

46. Colorado: *People v. Salinas,* 191 Colo. 171, 551 P.2d 703, 706 (1976).
    Hawaii: *Holdman v. Olim,* 59 Haw. 346, 581 P.2d 1164, 1168–69 (1978).
    Maryland: *Rand v. Rand,* 280 Md. 508, 374 A.2d 900, 903 (1977).
    Pennsylvania: *Commonwealth v. Butler,* 458 Pa. 289, 296, 328 A.2d 851, 855 (1974).
    Washington: *Darrin v. Gould,* 85 Wash.2d 859, 540 P.2d 882, 890 (1975).

47. Appendix B *infra* lists all state equal rights provisions and apparent standards of judicial review.

48. These states are Colorado, Hawaii, Maryland, Massachusetts, New Hampshire, New Mexico, Pennsylvania, Texas, and Washington. *See also* Appendix B *infra.*

49. These states are Connecticut, Hawaii, Illinois, and Montana. *See also* Appendix B *infra.*

50. Probably the best examples are the Maryland and Pennsylvania cases discussed below.

51. *People v. Salinas,* 191 Colo. 171, 551 P.2d 703 (1976); *People v. Banger,* 191 Colo. 152, 500 P.2d 1281 (1976).

52. *Singer v. Hara,* 11 Wash. App. 247, 522 P.2d 1187 (1974).

53. *Seattle v. Buchanan,* 90 Wash.2d 584, 584 P.2d 918 (1978).

54. *Holdman v. Olim,* 59 Haw. 346, 581 P.2d 1164 (1978). The Hawaii Supreme Court also relied on the unique physical characteristic qualification in upholding a directive that all women visitors entering the state prison must be wearing a brassiere.

55. 280 Md. 508, 374 A.2d 900 (1977).

56. 458 Pa. 97, 327 A.2d 60 (1974).

57. 85 Wash.2d 859, 540 P.2d 882 (1975).

58. 374 A.2d at 903–3.

59. 37 Md. App. 322, 377 A.2d 553 (1977).

60. *Id.* at 556.

61. 327 A.2d at 62.

62. 540 P.2d at 884.

63. *Id.* at 890.

64. *In re Hauser,* 15 Wash. App. 231, 548 P.2d 333, 337 (1976) (emphasis in original). *See,* however, *Singer v. Hara,* 11 Wash. App. 247, 522 P.2d 1187 (1974).

65. 540 P.2d at 893.

Chapter 7

1. *Senate Report, supra* note 15, ch. 4, at 13.

2. *House Hearings, supra* note 3, ch. 2, at 308.

3. *Id.*

4. *Id.* at 134.

5. *Id.* at 99.

6. *Senate Hearings, supra* note 23, ch. 5, at 320.

7. Brown, Emerson, *et al., supra* note 42, ch. 6, at 968.

8. *House Hearings, supra* note 3, ch. 2, at 163.

9. Brown, Emerson, *et al., supra* note 42, ch. 6, at 973.

10. *Senate Report, supra* note 15, ch. 4, at 13.

11. Professor Thomas I. Emerson of Yale Law School and the other people who wrote the Yale Law Journal article described by Senator Bayh, the chairman of the committee that wrote the Senate report, as "a masterly piece of scholarship."

12. *Senate Report, supra* note 15, ch. 4, at 13.

13. *Id.* at 14.

14. *See House Hearings, supra* note 3, ch. 2, at 165.

15. *Id.* at 328.

16. *Id.* at 134.

17. *Id.* at 164.

18. *Id.* at 163, 373–74.

19. *Id.* at 165. For other examples of dodging the combat issue, see *Id.* at 538 and 539 (Edith M. "Peggy" Parkey, President, Central Cincinnati Chapter,

Federally Employed Women, Inc.), and at 566 (Jacqueline G. Gutwillig, Chairman, Citizens' Advisory Council on the Status of Women).

20. Brown, Emerson, *et al.*, *supra* note 42, ch. 6, at 978.

21. *Id.* at 977.

22. *Senate Report*, *supra* note 15, ch. 4, at 37.

23. *See*, *e.g.*, Personnel *Administrator of Massachusetts v. Feeney*, 442 U.S. 256 (1979) and n.7 at 261.

24. Brown, Emerson, *et al.*, *supra* note 42, ch. 6, at 969.

25. *Id.*

26. It is possible that this same result may obtain under the Fourteenth Amendment. That issue is presented by two cases presently pending in the federal courts. In one, *Goldberg v. Rostker*, Civ. Action No. 71-1480 (E.D. Pa.) (filed in 1971), a three-judge district court ruled that under *Craig v. Boren* the registration requirement for men but not women violates the applicable judicial scrutiny test. Mr. Justice Brennan stayed enforcement of the Court's opinion pending possible review by the Supreme Court. The government's jurisdictional statement (petition for review of the case by the Supreme Court) has been filed and will be considered by the Court when it reconvenes in the fall of 1980.

The other case, *Barnett v. Rostker*, Civ. Action No. 80-1578 (D.D.C.) is pending before a single-judge court in the District of Columbia.

Chapter 8

1. *See* pp. 47–52 *supra*. For convenience, this standard will sometimes be referred to as the "qualified absolutist" standard.

2. *Senate Report*, *supra* note 15, ch. 4, at 16; *House Hearings*, *supra* note 3, ch. 2, at 40, 511, 566.

3. The American Law Institute, *Model Penal Code* at 142 (1962).

4. *See*, *e.g.*, Ala. Code §13-1-132; Ga. Code Ann. §26-2001; Hawaii Rev. Stat. §707-730(a); Idaho Code §18-6101; Ill. Ann. Stat. Ch. 38, §11-1 (Smith-Hurd); Miss. Code Ann. §97-3-65 and §97-3-67.

5. *See*, *e.g.*, Fla. Stat. Ann. §794.011 (West); Ind. Code Ann. §35-42-4-1 (Burns); Mich. Comp. Laws Ann. §750.520(a); N.M. Stat. Ann. §30-9-11; S.D. Codified Laws Ann. §22-22-1; Wash. Rev. Code Ann. §9.79.170.

6. Brown, Emerson, *et al.*, *supra* note 42, ch. 6, at 956.

7. *Id.*

8. *House Hearings*, *supra* note 3, ch. 2, at 433.

9. *See*, *e.g.*, Ga. Code Ann. §26-2018; Hawaii Rev. Stat. §707-730(b); Miss. Code Ann. §97-3-65 and §97-3-67.

10. *See*, *e.g.*, Ill. Ann. Stat. Ch. 38, §11-10 (*see* committee comments); Tenn. Code Ann. §39-706.

11. *See, e.g.,* Wis. Stat. Ann. §944.30 (West); La. Rev. Stat. Ann. §14.82 (West). As stated by the California Commission's *Commentary, supra* note 44, ch. 6, "there is little doubt that statutes which punish only female prostitutes will be unconstitutional after passage of an Equal Rights Amendment." (*Commentary* at 100). This statement is made against the background of the *Commentary's* conclusion that the qualified absolutist standard will govern the ERA. *Commentary* at 21. *See also, Holdman v. Olim,* 59 Hawaii 346, 581 P.2d 1164 (1978).

12. Note, *The Legality of Homosexual Marriage,* 82 Yale L.J. 573 (1973).

13. 11 Wash. App. 247, 522 P.2d 1187, 1193 (1974).

14. *House Hearings, supra* note 3, ch. 2, at 402.

15. *Id.*

16. 522 P.2d 1187.

17. *Extension Hearings, supra* note 31, ch. 6, at 123.

18. *House Hearings, supra* note 3, ch. 2, at 402.

19. *Id.*

20. *See* Lee, *supra* note 2, ch. 2, at chs. 12 & 18.

21. 410 U.S. 113 (1973).

22. See the exchange between Congressman Wiggins and Professor Emerson on this subject appearing in *House Hearings, supra* note 3, ch. 2, at 403–4.

23. *Pell v. Procunier,* 417 U.S. 817 (1974).

24. *House Report, supra* note 36, ch. 5, at 7.

Chapter 9

1. H. Clark, *Law of Domestic Relations in the United States,* §6.2 at 187 (1968).

2. *Id.* at 188.

3. Actually the Alabama statute gave the courts power or jurisdiction only to award alimony to wives (impose alimony obligations on husbands), rather than prohibit the imposition of alimony obligations on wives, though in effect it produced the same result.

4. 440 U.S. 268 (1979).

5. Clark, §15.1, *supra* note 1, at 488, 489.

6. Foster and Freed, *Life with Father: 1978,* 11 Fam. L.Q. 321 (1978).

7. Jones, *The Tender Years Doctrine: Survey and Analysis,* 16 J.Fam.L. 695 (1977–78).

8. *Id.* at 731–32.

9. There is one bit of testimony to the effect that presumptions favoring women in child custody cases would survive, but since the testimony is not only out of harmony with all other evidence but also internally inconsistent, it probably can be disregarded. *See House Hearings, supra* note 3, ch. 2, at 298–99.

10. *See generally Orr v. Orr, supra,* and *on remand,* 374 So.2d 895 (Ala. App. 1979), *appeal dismissed,* 100 S. Ct. 993 (1980).

11. In *Champlin Refining Co. v. Corporation Commission,* 286 U.S. 210, 234 (1932). The Supreme Court said: "The unconstitutionality of a part of an Act does not necessarily defeat or affect the validity of its remaining provisions. Unless it is evident that the legislature would not have enacted those provisions which are within its power, independently of that which is not, the invalid part may be dropped if what is left is fully operative as a law."

12. *Kneher v. Kneher,* 6 Fam.L.Rep. (BNA) 2195 (N.Y. Sup. Ct. 1980).

13. *House Hearings, supra* note 3, ch. 2, at 297.

14. *See, e.g., Linkletter v. Walker,* 381 U.S. 618 (1965), and *Phoenix v. Kolodziejski,* 399 U.S. 204 (1970).

15. This assumes that the courts would consider the prospectivity approach appropriate for implementing an amendment to the Constitution. There is no precedent either supporting or opposing such a position.

16. Although it is true that domicile is a traditional basis for divorce jurisdiction, many states have laws allowing resident nondomiciliaries (*e.g.,* resident military personnel with other domiciles) to file for divorce. *See* the Uniform Marriage and Divorce Act, §302(a) (1970).

17. Clark, §4.3, *supra* note 1, at 149, 150.

18. *See generally Id.* at 150–51.

19. Brown, Emerson, *et al., supra* note 42, ch. 6, at 871, 942.

20. Clark, §4.3, *supra* note 1, at 151. This rule applies when the parents are married and living together. Other rules apply when the parents are separated or divorced.

21. For a general discussion of these restrictive laws *see* L. Kanowitz, *supra* note 1, ch. 1, at ch. 3.

22. *See* pp. 2–3 *supra.*

23. W. Reppy and W. de Funiak, *Community Property in the United States,* 1–2 (1975). *See also id.* 1979 Cumulative Supplement at 29.

24. *Id.* at 1 (Supp. 1979).

25. *Id.* at 25–26, 296–98.

26. Brown, Emerson, *et al., supra* note 42, ch. 6, at 871, 940.

27. *Senate Report, supra* note 15, ch. 4, at 50.

28. *Id.*

29. Brown, Emerson, *et al., supra* note 42, ch. 6, at 871, 940.

Chapter 10

1. *House Hearings, supra* note 3, ch. 2, at 514.

2. *Senate Report, supra* note 15, ch. 4, at 15.

3. *House Hearings, supra* note 23, ch. 5, at 348, 565.

4. *Senate Report, supra* note 15, ch. 4, at 15.

5. *House Hearings, supra* note 23, ch. 5, at 212–15, 252–63, 332–36. The AFL-CIO initially opposed the amendment and then later changed its position to one of support.

6. *Id.* at 113, 123, 348, 569; *Senate Report, supra* note 15, ch. 4, at 15–16.

7. *Philbrook v. Glodgett,* 421 U.S. 707 (1975); *Pennsylvania R.R. v. U.S.,* 55 F.Supp. 473 (D.N.J. 1943), *aff'd* in part and *rev'd* in part, 323 U.S. 612 (1945); *Elizabeth Arden, Inc. v. Federal Trade Commission,* 156 F.2d 132 (2d Cir. 1946), *cert. denied,* 331 U.S. 806 (1947); *Darlington, Inc. v. Federal Housing Administration,* 142 F.Supp. 341 (E.D.S.C. 1956), *rev'd,* 352 U.S. 977 (1957); *U.S. v. Hougland Barge Line, Inc.,* 387 F.Supp. 1110 (W.D. Pa. 1974).

8. State courts interpreting state ERA provisions have divided on this issue. Compare *Scanlon v. Crim,* 500 S.W.2d 554 (Tex. Civ. App. 1973), with *Wiegand v. Wiegand,* 226 Pa. Super. Ct. 278, 310 A.2d 426 (1973).

9. 208 U.S. 412 (1908).

10. *Senate Report, supra* note 15, ch. 4, at 15.

11. *Id.* at 42.

12. 261 U.S. 525 (1923). *See* the discussion in ch. 4 *supra,* particularly note 36.

13. 42 U.S.C. §2000(e).

14. *Senate Report, supra* note 15, ch. 4, at 43–44.

15. *Babcock et al., supra* note 9, ch. 5, at 267–68, 270–72.

16. *House Hearings, supra* note 3, ch. 2, at 263.

17. *Id.* at 565.

18. It is possible, however, that under some circumstances private schools could be affected. In *Pennsylvania v. Board of Trustees,* 353 U.S. 230 (1957), the Supreme Court held that a school established by Stephen Girard's will for "poor white male orphans" could not exclude students on the basis of race. Though privately endowed, the school was administered, consistent with the terms of the will, by a board composed of city officials and persons designated by the local courts. After the Supreme Court's decision the state courts substituted private persons as trustees, but the United States Court of Appeals for the Third Circuit held that the substitution by the state courts made it unconstitutional state action. *Pennsylvania v. Brown,* 392 F.2d 120 (3rd Cir.), *cert. denied,* 391 U.S. 921 (1968). A similar result under similar circumstances should not result for single-sex schools under the Fourteenth Amendment because, as discussed in Chapter 4, the Fourteenth Amendment tests for gender-based discrimination and racial discrimination are not the same. Under the Equal Rights Amendment the constitutionality of a Girard-type school for "poor male orphans" would be doubtful.

19. *See* discussion at p. 88 *infra.*

20. 400 F.Supp. 326 (E.D. Pa. 1975), *rev'd,* 532 F.2d 880 (3d Cir. 1976), *aff'd* by an equally divided Court, 430 U.S. 703 (1977).

21. Mr. Justice Rehnquist was in the hospital, and the balance of the Court divided four and four on the issue.

22. For a more complete discussion of the *Vorchheimer* decision, *see infra* at 94. Two decades ago the Supreme Court declined to review a decision by the Texas Court of Civil Appeals upholding the exclusion of women from Texas A&M, a state college. *See Allred v. Heaton,* 336 S.W.2d 251, *appeal dismissed and cert. denied,* 364 U.S. 517 (1960), *rehearing denied,* 364 U.S. 944 (1961). *See also Heaton v. Bristol,* 317 S.W.2d 86 (1958), *appeal dismissed and cert. denied,* 359 U.S. 230, *rehearing denied,* 359 U.S. 999 (1959); *Williams v. McNair,* 401 U.S. 951 (1971) *aff'g* 316 F. Supp. 134 (D.J.C. 1970).

23. 85 Wash.2d 859, 549 P.2d 882 (1975).

24. *Id.* at 889.

25. *See also Commonwealth v. Pennsylvania Interscholastic Athletic Ass'n.,* 18 PaC Commw. Ct. 45, 334 A.2d 839 (1975), where the Pennsylvania Commonwealth Court ordered that the Pennsylvania Interscholastic Athletic Association (PIAA) "permit girls to practice and compete with boys in interscholastic athletics," including contact football (*Id.* at 843). In so ordering, the court held that "the existence of certain characteristics to a greater degree in one sex does not justify classification by sex rather than by the particular characteristic." (*Id.*)

26. *Equal Rights Amendment Extension*: Hearings on H.J. Res. 638 before the Subcomm. on Civil and Constitutional Rights of the House Comm. on the Judiciary, 95th Cong., 1st and 2d Sess. 364 (1977-78).

27. *Women's Educational Equity Act of 1973*: Hearings on S. 2518 before the Subcomm. on Education of the Senate Comm. on Labor and Public Welfare, 93d Cong., 1st Sess. 303-4, 309, 318 (1973).

28. These issues arise under Section 901(a) of the Education Amendments of 1972 (20 U.S.C. §1681 [1976]) and HEW's implementing regulations, 45 C.F.R. §86.23(a), §86.37(c), and §86.41.

29. There is also an issue concerning the reach of regulating authority. In 1976 the NCAA filed suit against HEW, asserting that HEW has no authority to issue or enforce Title IX regulations that would govern intercollegiate athletic programs receiving no federal assistance. In 1978 the U.S. District Court for the District of Kansas held that this issue was not ripe for judicial consideration because no "administrative decision has been formalized and its effects felt in a concrete way by the challenging parties." *NCAA v. Califano,* 444 F.Supp. 425, 439 (D.Kan. 1978), citing *Abbott Laboratories v. Gardner,* 387 U.S. 136, 148 (1966). The District Court also held that the NCAA did not have standing to sue. On appeal, on April 17, 1980, the U.S. Court of Appeals for the Tenth Circuit held that the NCAA did have standing to sue, and the case was reversed and remanded. *NCAA v. Califano,* No. 78-1632, Slip op. (10th Cir. Apr. 17, 1980).

Chapter 11

1. *See* chs. 2 & 3 *supra.*

2. *See supra,* note 16, ch. 5.

3. *Goesaert v. Cleary*, 335 U.S. 464 (1948).

4. *House Hearings, supra* note 3, ch. 2, at 50, 357.

5. *Id.* at 90, 123.

6. 404 U.S. 71 (1971). *Reed v. Reed* was decided November 22, 1971. The House passed the ERA on October 12, 1971, and the Senate on March 22, 1972.

7. *See generally* ch. 4 *supra* and app. A *infra*.

8. 118 Cong. Rec. 8902, 92d Cong. 2d Sess., 1972; *House Hearings, supra* note 3, ch. 2, at 90, 167, 361.

9. Professor Paul Freund states:

> The value of a symbol, however, lies precisely in the fact that it is not to be taken literally, that it is not meant to be analysed closely for its exact implications. A concurrent resolution of Congress, expressing the general sentiment of that body, would be an appropriate vehicle for promulgating a symbol. When, however, we are presented with a proposed amendment to our fundamental law, binding on federal and state governments, on judges, legislature, and executives, we are entitled to inquire more circumspectly into the operational meaning and effects of the symbol. Freund, *The Equal Rights Amendment is Not the Way.* Reprinted in *House Hearings, supra* note 3, ch. 2, at 607, 610.

10. 20 U.S.C. §1681(a)(8) (1976).

11. *See* Lee, *supra* note 2, ch. 2, at ch. 2.

12. *See Reopening an Old Debate*, 115 Time 32 (Feb. 11, 1980) and *Registration Plan Cheered, Booed*, 88 U.S. News and World Report 7 (Feb. 18, 1980).

13. Wash. Post, Feb. 20, 1980, at A1, col. 1; Wash. Post, March 7, 1980, at A7, col. 1.

14. *See Nebbia v. New York*, 291 U.S. 502, 524 (1934), citing the *License Cases*, 46 U.S. (5 How.) 504, 583 (1847).

15. *See generally* ch. 9 *supra*.

16. *See* Lee, *supra* note 2, ch. 2, at ch. 6.

17. The Equal Pay Act prohibits discrimination on the basis of sex so far as equal pay for equal work is concerned. *See* 29 U.S.C.A. §206 (1963).

18. The best discussion of this subject in the legislative history is in the minority views of Congressman Edward Hutchinson. *See House Report, supra* note 36, ch. 5, at 13–16.

19. *See generally* Brown, Emerson, *et al., supra* note 42, ch. 6, at 908.

20. *See* Lee, *supra* note 2, ch. 2, at ch. 6 for a general discussion of federal and state powers. For some congressional views concerning the effect of Section 2 on state-federal relationships, see the remarks of Congressman Mikva, a proponent, *House Hearings, supra* note 3, ch. 2, at 91–92, and Senator Ervin, an opponent, 118 Cong. Rec. 9081 (1972). *See also* L. Tribe, *American Constitutional Law* 1075 (1978).

21. Section 2 of the Equal Rights Amendment also creates the possibility of a power shift from the federal judiciary to the federal Congress. Though the exact reach of the cases is uncertain, the Supreme Court has interpreted the enforcement provision of the Fourteenth Amendment (Section 5) as giving Congress at least some role in declaring principles of constitutional law. *See South Carolina v. Katzenbach,* 383 U.S. 301 (1966); *Katzenbach v. Morgan,* 384 U.S. 641 (1966); and *Oregon v. Mitchell,* 400 U.S. 112 (1970). Whatever the result of Section 2 in this respect, it is quite clear that the net effect of the ERA as an allocator of power between the courts and legislatures will favor the courts. That is, the shift of policymaking authority from the legislatures to the courts under Section 1 would be greater than the shift of authority under Section 2 from the courts to Congress to say what the ERA means.

22. *Allgeyer v. Louisiana,* 165 U.S. 578 (1897); *Lochner v. New York,* 198 U.S. 45 (1905); *Adair v. United States,* 208 U.S. 161 (1908); *Coppage v. Kansas,* 236 U.S. 1 (1915); *Adkins v. Children's Hospital,* 261 U.S. 525 (1923).

23. *See* discussion of abortion cases in app. A *infra. See also* Lee, *supra* note 2, ch. 2, at chs. 17–18.

24. *Allgeyer v. Louisiana,* 165 U.S. 578 (1897).

25. *Id.*

26. *See* Lee, *supra* note 2, ch. 2, at ch. 17.

27. Any chances for correction would surely be destroyed by passage of the Equal Rights Amendment, which would also seal the fate of the few remaining peripheral abortion questions, such as spousal and parental notification of the abortion decision and postviability abortion regulation.

Appendix A

1. 368 U.S. 57 (1961). For a discussion of this case, *see* p. 25 *supra.*

2. For an explanation of why the case involved the Fifth Amendment and not the Fourteenth Amendment, *see* note 12, ch. 4 *supra* and note 1, ch. 2 *supra.*

3. 430 U.S. at 223.

4. The Court applied the rule from *Craig v. Boren,* that "classifications by gender must serve important governmental objectives and must be substantially related to the achievement of those objectives." 429 U.S. at 197. *See* pp. 27–28 *supra.*

5. 442 U.S. at 230.

6. *See* note 2 *supra.*

7. U.S. Const. art. I, §6.

8. 440 U.S. at 269.

9. 443 U.S. at 77.

10. 419 U.S. at 498.

11. R. Ginsburg, *Sex Equality and the Constitution,* 52 Tul.L.Rev. 451, 465–66 (1978).

12. 42 U.S.C. §415(b)(3) (1970 & Supp. II 1972).

13. *See* Lee, *supra* note 2, ch. 2, at ch. 14.

14. *Washington v. Davis,* 426 U.S. 229 (1976); *Arlington Heights v. Metropolitan House Development Corp.,* 429 U.S. 252 (1977).

15. *See* Lee, *supra* note 2, ch. 2, at ch. 15.

16. 42 U.S.C. §2000(e).

17. *See, e.g.,* Ginsburg, *supra* note 11, at 462.

18. 42 U.S.C. §2000(e).

Table of Cases
(with page references to this volume)

134

Index